MY PASSION FOR WATER

Michael Palin, Ann Widdecombe, Sir Ranulph Fiennes and many others
share memories of their favourite oceans, seas and rivers

IN AID OF

Just a drop
Safe Water = Saved Lives

NOBLE CALEDONIA

This edition published by James Pembroke Publishing Ltd
& Noble Caledonia in 2011

First published in 2011
by James Pembroke Publishing Ltd
90 Walcot Street
Bath BA1 5BG
www.jppublishing.co.uk

ISBN: 978-1-901170-18-4

A catalogue record for this book is available from the British Library

Printed and bound in the UK by Butler Tanner & Dennis

*A tabular iceberg floating within
Paradise Harbour, Antarctica*

In celebration of 20 years of Noble Caledonia

Contents

An Uros woman navigates the waters of Lake Titicaca, Peru on a totora reed boat

Rekindling memories of a bygone age on the deck of Sea Cloud II

Water, the gift of life

Welcome to *My Passion for Water*, a celebration of fun and adventure on – or sometimes just next to – some of the world's most remote, surprising or simply enjoyable seas and rivers. Within its pages, a wide range of celebrities, writers and travel experts pick the water-related moments that have meant the most to them, for reasons moving, personal or just plain hilarious (Johnny Ball struggling manfully with French canal bridges springs to mind). We thank them all.

Of course, the reason this book exists in the first place is to celebrate the first 20 years of Noble Caledonia, the small ship cruise specialist offering a striking and unusual range of tours aimed at the more seasoned and adventurous traveller. For all at Noble, the last two decades have been a fruitful and enjoyable period, as we've steadily spread our net wider, taking our small ship and river cruising trips to every continent. In doing so, we hope to have enriched the lives of all who've travelled with us, offering a learning experience as well as a holiday.

Perhaps, on occasion, we have been guilty of taking some of these wonderful experiences for granted, but – if so – this has never been the case for very long: always, just around the corner, lies something new to open our eyes and minds, be it a region (the old Soviet Union, say) opening up to us, or the way the extensive spaces of the Arctic or Antarctic seem to demand we consider the bigger issues. The first-hand experience of the very different (and often highly challenging) ways in which life is lived in far corners of the globe rarely fails to make a very personal impact. But often it is by seeing the familiar as others see it – a cruise experienced through the prism of our on-ship experts, say – that a place or experience really comes to life.

This book, in its own small way, hopes to be similarly eye-opening.

The 20 years of Noble Caledonia have seen the travel opportunities afforded to many of us expand phenomenally, but something else comes hand-in-hand with this privilege: a sense of responsibility. This could be for our environment, or for those less fortunate souls scraping a living in some barren land. Modern communication brings these realities into our lives daily, but it is often through direct experience that they really start to mean something to us.

Water is vital to Noble Caledonia – but it can be especially easy to take it for granted. Not so for many less fortunate. As we finalise this book that celebrates water, we hear of another drought-inflicted famine in the Horn of Africa. The charity Just a Drop has found a place in the hearts of many worldwide travel and tourism organisations for its work in water aid projects, and it is to this noble endeavour that we dedicate *My Passion for Water*.

Andrew Cochrane
Managing Director, Noble Caledonia

The very essence of life

Just a rop
Safe Water = Saved Lives

Just a Drop works to combat waterborne disease, the biggest killer of young children worldwide

Moved by the plight of so many children throughout the world to whom clean water is still a luxury, not a right, the founders of Just a Drop launched the charity with a wide-reaching remit. Today, it raises desperately needed funds to build wells, install boreholes and hand pumps worldwide, and run health and sanitation programmes that offer our children the most precious gift on Earth, the chance of a healthy life.

The need remains a pressing one. Polluted water is the planet's single biggest killer of children under the age of five. Over 1.4 million children still die every year – that's one every 20 seconds – from waterborne diseases such as cholera, dysentery and diarrhoea; these are caused by either the complete lack of access to fresh water, or the pollution of whatever water is available.

My Passion for Water celebrates the joy that water can bring, and the good memories that it generates. However, for far too many its very absence has the most awful of consequences. It is the very essence of life: we can survive a month without food, but only three days without water.

Working with a team of in-field volunteers – including qualified engineers and project officers – as well as properly evaluated local NGOs (non-governmental organisations), Just a Drop's Trustees assess a wide range of proposals. Many of these affect some of the poorest and most remote communities in the world. Each potential project is checked in its country of origin, and every aspect is carefully scrutinised prior to money being committed. Of vital importance is the ongoing sustainability and maintenance of a project.

Just a Drop is a charity with global reach. However, when undertaking projects anywhere in the world where there's a genuine need, the organisation has a real determination to keep front and centre the individual nature of what we do. To this end, we're constantly looking to ensure that the way we use your money has direct and measurable benefit to children and families in need. At the same time, great effort is also made to build links between our donors and our beneficiaries. After all, when you've made a genuine difference to people's lives, it's extremely satisfying to be able to see exactly how.

What has Just a Drop achieved?
Since it was launched in 1998, Just a Drop has supported over one million people in over 30 countries around the world, building wells in countries including: Afghanistan, Bangladesh, Bolivia, Cambodia, Chile, Ecuador, Ethiopia, India, Indonesia, Kenya, Malawi, Mongolia, Morocco, Mozambique, Nicaragua, Niger, Philippines, Sri Lanka, Sudan, Swaziland, Tanzania, Uganda, Zambia and Zimbabwe.

We've also undertaken emergency relief work, helping victims of floods in Mozambique and supporting earthquake victims in Turkey; we funded a massive health and sanitation programme in Southern Africa too, and completed a project in Grenada following Hurricane Ivan. We're currently working in Haiti, helping to rebuild the water infrastructure in schools after the devastating earthquake of January 2010.

For more information on projects supported by Just a Drop, please go to our website: www.justadrop.org

How can you help?
If you wish to donate to Just a Drop, please visit www.justgiving.com/justadrop/donate. Alternatively, please contact Ana Sustelo at ana.sustelo@reedexpo.co.uk.

Europe

Awe-inspiring landscapes, remains of ancient
civilizations and historic monuments unfold along
Europe's coastline, rivers and canals

The Chain Bridge, which spans the River Danube between the eastern and western sides of Budapest

Square-rigger
off Cape Trafalgar

A s a colonial boy I first took notice of the sea in 1956, when rackety liners like the Stirling Castle were still the main means of travel from the southern hemisphere to Britain.

The SS Rajula was not so much rackety as rickety. Although built in the '20s, she was still plying between Madras and Penang in 1972, when for some of us the old hippie trail ran to Australia. She took a week to cross the Bay of Bengal. One evening a projector was set up and, while we sprawled on the deck, scenting the rare blend of sea and cannabis, it rattled off a four-reeler: *Waterloo*.

Five years ago, I was researching a book set in the age of sail and, to get some understanding of how men used to work the tops, I took a voyage in a square-rigger of the Sail Training Association. My son joined me.

Nearing Gibraltar, we tumbled from our hammocks before dawn, made our way to the bow and went out on nets cradled beneath the boom. We found ourselves passing over the waters off Cape Trafalgar on a two-master. Somehow we were alone – except that just then five smooth bodies appeared off the bow, rising and disappearing with the waves. Then the dolphins began to perform – frolicking, spinning and diving. We waved and, because we were happy, we smiled. They smiled back, then accelerated, crossing the bow and performing a victory roll beneath us, before they disappeared. ●

Stephen Taylor
Journalist
and author

Lighthouse at Cape Trafalgar in Cadiz, the site of the famous naval battle in 1805

Écréhous Islands English Channel

O n a clear day you can see the Écréhous from the end of the pier at Gorey Castle. The islands are mid way between Jersey and the coast of Brittany, not much more than a group of granite rocks that have managed to surface above the waves, but to me, they're one of the most magical places on earth.

I first went there when I was 13. My mother was a Jersey girl, and some childhood friends of hers owned two fishermen's huts. We set sail soon after breakfast, heading due east into the swell. I was horribly sick and failed to notice the islands getting closer and larger until we were dropping anchor in the sheltered bay between the two largest. It was an hour or so to go before full low tide, but the strange moonscape of gulleys, shell-strewn beaches and pools seemed to stretch for miles. We rowed our stuff ashore in dinghies then carried the bags, boxes and water containers up the steep hill to the group of huts, clustered together around the top of the rocky outcrop. Sixteen or so, all about ten feet wide and 13 feet long, looking out towards the ever changing sea; they were rough and basic, yet for the old Jersey families, these odd-shaped little dwellings meant as much as any family stately home.

Along with two other teenage girls, I was allocated

Rosie Boycott
Journalist, author
and broadcaster

a camp bed in the attic. It was hot and stuffy and completely fabulous. I could peer out of the little window and watch the waves, the seals, the sea birds screeching overhead. Sickness forgotten, we tucked into hard-boiled eggs, tomatoes, ham and salad dressing, all squashed around the dining table which took up most of the ground floor of the hut. After lunch, it was time for swimming and exploring. Armed with fishing nets we went off to get dinner: fat prawns shaken from their roosts under waving seaweed banks, pink crabs, a couple of plaice scooped from their hiding place in the sand, wonky-shaped oysters bashed off rocks.

Later, as the sun started to set, we sat with mugs of hot chocolate watching the tide power inwards, lapping over the rocks, creeping over the jetty, moving up the beach below the fishermen's huts. At low tide, we could walk to the other rocks; now they were their own islands. At high tide, we were alone on our tiny world, a world which would fit easily into half a football pitch. As darkness fell, the surrounding sea seemed to be gently rocking us to sleep. I slept that night as though awake in a dream world and, the following morning, in that moment between sleeping and waking, when I still hadn't opened my eyes, I wondered if I had indeed dreamed the whole thing. I prayed frantically that I had not. It was a great relief to open my eyes. ●

Casquets Lighthouse
off Alderney, north of
the Écréhous islands

French canal holidays

Our best ever holiday at sea was on a gulet boat out of Turkey in the very first year that Thomson holidays offered them. As well as being the best, it was the cheapest holiday in the catalogue. Our two boys of around 11 and 12 loved it – and I finally had to learn how to swim!

But what you'd doubtless like to hear about are the two most horrendous boat holidays we ever had – both, as it happens, out of Agde, the French port known as 'the Black Pearl of the Mediterranean' thanks to its distinctive black basalt monuments. The first was along the wonderful Canal du Midi, and would have been idyllic had the two-bit firm of boat hirers not given us a petrol-engined boat that required a desperate search for fuel every second day, gave constant spark plug trouble, and had an engine so underpowered I could not keep it away from the bank in a mild wind. But we did eventually get to the beautiful fortified town of Carcassonne – the last three miles by taxi.

So, a couple of years later, we tried again. For this second trip we planned to head east into the Camargue,

Johnny Ball
TV presenter
and author

and this time our boat was brand new and spotless. The problem was there was a major lock closed for repair, so going east was not an option – unless we motored the first bit to pick up an identical boat near Montpelier. No problem? You wouldn't think so – except this second boat was dirty, ancient and in terrible condition. After tears from my wife Di and my daughter Zoe, we decided we had no alternative, so we took the boat and set off. Within the week we'd made Arles and its double-decker Roman aqueduct, as well as the tiny walled city of Aigues-Mortes (Pain of Death), where the Children's Crusade is said to have sailed from (though it is now some seven kilometres inland). There we had a sumptuous banquet of seafood, all of it unexpectedly raw. Delicious, but it's quite a strain on the nerves eating sea snails and mussels that wriggle when lemon juice is squirted onto them!

The Camargue can be very flat and a bit boring, so we found a side canal that leads to Les Saintes-Maries. Problem was, a low bridge and a sign saying 'No House Boats' barred the way. Naturally, we decided the sign wasn't meant for us – after all, we could see houseboats moored along the bank on the other side.

The sun's rays peek through the trees along the idyllic Canal du Midi in the south of France

As it turned out, the clearance between the bridge and the sun-roof on our boat was no more than two inches, but we squeezed through and tootled along, heading south. As we progressed, we passed more and more moored boats – and fewer and fewer spaces. But surely, I thought, there will be a good one soon, and handy for the small town that we were approaching.

Then we realised that we were going faster. The current was increasing rapidly, and ahead we saw a low, and very old, double-arched bridge. Two canal spurs, one from each side, joined our canal here, and it seemed that this is what was causing our faster pace. The three canals seemed to be gushing under the bridge and heading for the sea.

I tried to turn, and was doing well, until the current overtook us and the boat slammed – more than a little violently – against the bridge. Our boat couldn't really pass under the bridge, but the current was holding us to it, the noise of the water now all around us.

Above us, local people were shouting advice and suggesting we were "stupid English", but I shouted above them, "Don't listen to them, listen to me!" With Di at the

wheel, a long pole between my chest and the brickwork, and in a high state of pain and anguish, I managed to push the front end away from the bridge. When I had made the gap as wide as possible, I shouted to Di to give it full throttle forward, turning only ever so slightly right. We made it at the second attempt and, at very slow speed, headed back the way we had come. Relieved, we found a vacant bit of bank and moored up for the night.

We were all in shock. That night my wife, daughter Zoe and sons Nick and Dan 'sent me to Coventry' and played board games without me – and rightly so. We went to bed early, which was just as well because at first light we were awakened by the most almighty din. Just what was causing the noise wasn't clear but, after a few minutes – and as the racket increased in volume – I got to the towpath and climbed a bank of around eight feet high.

As I got to the top, my mouth dropped open. I turned and shouted for the others to come and look. They joined me quickly, and we gazed in amazement across salt flats stretching east towards the rising sun. There, flapping, dabbling and squawking to greet the start of another day, were around two million fabulous pink flamingos. ●

Flamingos by sunset in the Camargue region between Arles and Saintes Maries de la Mer

Flotilla of Turkish gulets

While I was an undergraduate at Oxford, I went on a flotilla holiday on traditional two-masted gulets. It was a confluence of the Jay and Johnson tribes, and burningly hot. We set off from Dalaman in Turkey, and visited Roman ruins and tavernas. Pale-skinned Johnsons fought over scraps of shade so that we could read our books while caramel-coloured Jays, with sinuous, oiled brown limbs, scampered around doing things with sheets and ticking us off for calling them 'ropes'.

Peter Jay, the most senior person on board both in age and yachtie terms, wore a peaked hat emblazoned with the words 'Capt Jay', and brought a new wife – the flashing-eyed Emma – and baby boy Tommy, as well as his own elegant, mahogany-hulled yacht called Norvantes. He also wore blue cotton pyjamas, which

Rachel Johnson
Editor of *The Lady*,
author and columnist

flapped open in the breeze around the fly area. But that was nothing as the captain of my gulet, Nelson Mews, a TV producer, together with his wife Julie, wore no clothes whatsoever for two weeks. I spent much of my time trying to avoid following them up companionways – it was simply too much to cope with as a poncey undergraduate.

Martin Jay was also there, and at one point he visited a mud bath. I still have a picture of Martin covered with the stuff in my album, as well as a picture of Alice Jay, daughter of Peter, topless while at the helm of Norvantes. With this crew, I hope you can understand why I remember very little of the actual sailing we did. What sticks in the mind is that it was incredibly hot and the sky was incredibly blue. Afterwards I decided I would never go on a small boat again, and especially not with naturists in their fifties. And I haven't. ●

A gulet leisure boat on the crystal blue waters of the Turkish Mediterranean

Ferry to Ibiza

Back in the 1970s we would take the Barcelona ferry when visiting Uncle Christopher in Ibiza. Ferries arrived in the early morning and people would rush to the port to watch. Ships left in the early evening. Passengers would hold one end of a loo roll and throw the roll down, to be seized by loved ones on land. As the ferry pulled away, hundreds of streamers would spool, tauten and break, floating into the blue waters.

Christopher was ex-Army, a bachelor, great fun but prone to flashes of rage. He thought women were hopeless. One year my teenage sister Melinda was staying behind with him for another week. She and 'C' were on the quayside waving us goodbye when Melinda remembered that my father still had her passport. Frantic shouts and gesticulations. The ferry had already started to move. We could see Christopher exploding at Melinda: "You bloody fool!" Daddy threw the passport from the deck. I remember the churning waters, the streamers, Spanish aftershave, then the slow arc of Mindy's passport, a glinting cartwheel through the Balearic evening air until it was caught by a suddenly ecstatic Christopher. "Olé!" cried the entire quayside. ●

Quentin Letts
Parliamentary sketch
writer, theatre critic
and author

*Early morning
in the port of Ibiza*

Schooner off Istanbul

t was 1968 and I was filming *The Charge of the Light Brigade* in Turkey. During the weeks that we were to film the British Army landings, we were based in Istanbul. My friend, David Hemmings, with his wife-to-be Gail Honeycutt, invited my wife Sue and I to live with them on a schooner that had been hired for the duration. It was a magnificent three-master, all teak and brass. (David said it had belonged to the President of Turkey – but then David might say anything.)

There was a state room, bedrooms, and, of course, a crew. We were anchored in the Sea of Marmara, right opposite the Topkapi Palace. One night, David and I took the bum-boat to the bar of the harbour hotel, where the rest of the film crew were staying. While having a drink there was a tremendous rumbling, and everything in the bar began to shake, with bottles and glasses crashing. My God, we thought, that must have been a very heavy lorry that passed by.

Suddenly into the bar came naked and half-naked people from the upper storeys of the hotel, screaming "Get out into the street". It was, of course, an earthquake. David and I rushed as quickly as we could across the heaving road to our little bum-boat and headed towards the schooner, which we could see as its lamps were lit. We managed to clamber aboard despite the churning sea, and then became aware that the whole of Istanbul was in complete darkness. The only sound was that of water slapping against the sides of the schooner. It made world news, but to the relief of our friends and relatives, we were safe. ●

Peter Bowles
TV and stage actor

View across Istanbul harbour towards the majestical Blue Mosque and Hagia Sophia

Rowing on
the River Thames

When we were small, my dad used to hire a rowing boat in the shadow of Halfpenny Bridge at Lechlade and row my brother and I upstream along the wandering upper reaches of the Thames. The journeys became part of our summers and were amongst the most thrilling of all. There were patches of yellow water lilies in still backwaters, willow herb and purple loosestrife on the banks, and occasionally the tiny turquoise flash of a kingfisher. We used to swim in deep pools under the willows, mud oozing through our toes as we clambered out onto the meadow's edge. Further upstream there was a footbridge across the river from which local boys would leap or swing from ropes into the water and flabbergast us with their bravery.

We skirted the weeping willows near the Round House, where the River Cole and the Thames and Severn Canal met the Thames. Sometimes the narrowing river grew so shallow that the boat dragged across the muddy bottom, and we had to push off from the bank with an oar to reach the midstream channel and our final mooring place beside the farm at Inglesham. We used to walk up through the yard to the squat, ancient church on its mild rise, overlooking the grassy undulations of a lost village across the lane. The journey back was swift. The sound of the oars plopping into the water and the quiet whoosh of the downstream drift between has never left me. It will forever epitomise the best of summer. ●

Candida Lycett Green
Columnist, author and contributing editor of *Vogue*

*Halfpenny Bridge on the River Thames
in Lechlade, Gloucestershire*

The North **Sea**

As a child I would walk a short way into the sea, stand still and talk to it, ten to the dozen, as if to a close friend. Now, much later, I listen. The friendship is more complex, more demanding.

The North Sea finally seduced me during the pause between making my sculpture *Scallop* and its full-scale realisation on Aldeburgh beach, Suffolk. Early in the morning of 30 November 2002, I experienced a dramatic storm: huge waves crashing on the beach, thrashing the shingle. Back in the studio, while working on a portrait from memory of a London beggar, I looked out to witness the landscape around me still ravaged by wind and rain. The urge to paint the experience of the morning took over and the sea surplanted the beggar on that canvas. This was the first of my North Sea paintings.

The North Sea, often like a raging beast, is eating away and changing the shoreline forever. As I get older I identify with the shifting shingle as time, like the sea, enforces an inevitable erosion. But this raging beast is as demanding as a lover and I am still seduced and challenged. ●

Maggi Hambling CBE
Contemporary painter, sculptor and printmaker

Wave Returning, oil on canvas, by Maggi Hambling (2009)

The Wind in the Willows

He thought his happiness was complete when, as he meandered aimlessly along, suddenly he stood by the edge of a full-fed river. Never in his life had he seen a river before – this sleek, sinuous, full-bodied animal, chasing and chuckling, gripping things with a gurgle and leaving them with a laugh, to fling itself on fresh playmates that shook themselves free, and were caught and held again. All was a-shake and a-shiver – glints and gleams and sparkles, rustle and swirl, chatter and bubble. The Mole was bewitched, entranced, fascinated. By the side of the river he trotted as one trots, when very small, by the side of a man who holds one spellbound by exciting stories; and when tired at last, he sat on the bank, while the river still chattered on to him, a babbling procession of the best stories in the world, sent from the heart of the earth to be told at last to the insatiable sea.

As he sat on the grass and looked across the river, a dark hole in the bank opposite, just above the water's edge, caught his eye, and dreamily he fell to considering what a nice snug dwelling-place it would make for an animal with few wants and fond of a bijou riverside residence, above flood level and remote from noise and dust. As he gazed, something bright and small seemed to twinkle down in the heart of it, vanished, then twinkled once more like a tiny star. But it could hardly be a star in such an unlikely situation; and it was too glittering and small

Kenneth Grahame
(1859-1932)

for a glow-worm. Then, as he looked, it winked at him, and so declared itself to be an eye; and a small face began gradually to grow up round it, like a frame round a picture. A brown little face, with whiskers. A grave round face, with the same twinkle in its eye that had first attracted his notice. Small neat ears and thick silky hair. It was the Water Rat! Then the two animals stood and regarded each other cautiously. "Hullo, Mole!" said the Water Rat. "Hullo, Rat!" said the Mole.

"Would you like to come over?" enquired the Rat presently.

"Oh, it's all very well to *talk*," said the Mole, rather pettishly, he being new to a river and riverside life and its ways. The Rat said nothing, but stooped and unfastened a rope and hauled on it; then lightly stepped into a little boat which the Mole had not observed. It was painted blue outside and white within, and was just the size for two animals; and the Mole's whole heart went

out to it at once, even though he did not yet fully understand its uses.

The Rat sculled smartly across and made fast. Then he held up his forepaw as the Mole stepped gingerly down. "Lean on that!" he said. "Now then, step lively!" and the Mole to his surprise and rapture found himself actually seated in the stern of a real boat.

"This has been a wonderful day!" said he, as the Rat shoved off and took to the sculls again. "Do you know, I've never been in a boat before in all my life."

"What?" cried the Rat, open-mouthed: "Never been in a – you never – well I – what have you been doing, then?"

"Is it so nice as all that?" asked the Mole shyly, though he was quite prepared to believe it as he leant back in his seat and surveyed the cushions, the oars, the rowlocks, and all the fascinating fittings, and felt the boat sway lightly under him.

"Nice? It's the *only* thing," said the Water Rat solemnly, as he leant forward for his stroke. "Believe me, my young friend, there is *nothing* – absolute nothing – half so much worth doing as simply messing about in boats. Simply messing," he went on dreamily: "messing – about – in – boats; messing..."

"Look ahead, Rat!" cried the Mole suddenly.

It was too late. The boat struck the bank full tilt. The dreamer, the joyous oarsman, lay on his back at the bottom of the boat, his heels in the air.

"...about in boats – or *with* boats," the Rat went on composedly, picking himself up with a pleasant laugh. "In or out of 'em, it doesn't matter. Nothing seems really to matter, that's the charm of it. Whether you get away, or whether you don't; whether you arrive at your destination or whether you reach somewhere else, or whether you never get anywhere at all, you're always busy, and you never do anything in particular; and when you've done it there's always something else to do, and you can do it if you like, but you'd much better not. Look here! If you've really nothing else on hand this morning, supposing we drop down the river together, and have a long day of it?"

The Mole waggled his toes from sheer happiness, spread his chest with a sigh of full contentment, and leaned back blissfully into the soft cushions. "*What* a day I'm having!" he said. "Let us start at once!"

"Hold hard a minute, then!" said the Rat. He looped the painter through a ring in his landing-stage, climbed up into his hole above, and after a short interval reappeared staggering under a fat, wicker luncheon-basket.

"Shove that under your feet," he observed to the Mole, as he passed it down into the boat. Then he untied the painter and took the sculls again.

"What's inside it?" asked the Mole, wriggling with curiosity.

"There's cold chicken inside it," replied the Rat briefly, "cold chicken, cold tongue, cold ham, cold beef, pickled gherkins, salad, French rolls, cress sandwiches, potted meat, ginger beer, lemonade, soda water..."

"O stop, stop," cried the Mole in ecstasies. "This is too much!" "Do you really think so?" enquired the Rat seriously. "It's only what I always take on these little excursions, and the other animals are always telling me that I'm a mean beast and cut it *very* fine!" ●

Asia

Ancient and modern collide as ornate gilded pavilions, sacred temples and Oriental treasures co-exist with futuristic skyscrapers, man-made wonders and bustling street markets

Exploring the Sundarbans

Some years ago I found myself on board a small boat in the waterways of the Sundarbans, the mangrove forest along the Bay of Bengal that embraces the greatest tidal delta in the world. The Sundarbans covers 2,300 square miles, two-fifths in India and three-fifths in Bangladesh. The forest, largely impenetrable on land, is cross-hatched by a network of waterways. Along these our small boat broke trail amongst densely packed sudari trees, a type of mangrove yielding wood suitable for telegraph poles and paper pulp. Primeval horseshoe crabs with rotating proboscises roamed the beaches, and the trees and banks teemed with life. The kingfishers alone had mutated into hundreds of species.

One day, before the monkeys woke, a gondola-shaped vessel emerged from the mist. As it glided silently past, I saw a pair of otters, harnessed and squeaking, dive through the milk chocolate water. On deck, four men manoeuvred nets attached to six-foot bamboo poles. It turns out that generations of Bengalis have trained otters to chase fish in the lonely backwaters of the Sundarbans. ●

Sara Wheeler
Travel writer, author
and biographer

*Fishing trawlers in the
Sundarbans, Bangladesh –
the world's largest tidal delta*

Sara Wheeler photo: Niall McDiarmid

The Indonesian
Archipelago

The year was 1974, and I remember we had some difficulty removing the large orangutan brought on board our Royal Navy patrol craft – goodness knows how – by one of my sailors in the middle of the night. We left on time from the steamy, somewhat ramshackle, port of Surabaya, with its flotilla of rusting and abandoned ex-Soviet warships.

Sailing onto a glass-smooth sea past Madura, we left Bali to starboard and entered the Java Sea surrounded by a fleet of elegant perahu, their sails hanging limply waiting for the first morning breeze. We headed for the Makassar Strait between Sulawesi and Borneo. Here the current against us increased to about three knots but, more alarmingly, our lookouts had to keep a sharp eye out for huge tree trunks felled by loggers and thrown into the sea to be collected at the strait's southern end.

Past Palau and into the Celebes Sea, we had no fear of the pirates who infested these waters because we were a warship, however small. Then we made the idyllic little port of Zamboanga on the southwestern tip of Mindanao, on the boundary between the Celebes and Sulu Seas, with thoughts of buttered lobster and steamed rice, luscious fruits and friendly locals. ●

Admiral Lord Alan West
Former First Sea Lord and Commander in Chief of the Royal Navy, and former Under-Secretary for Security, Counter-terrorism and Police

A traditional Filipino outrigger fishing boat (banka) on a white sand beach in the Philippines

Picnic at Sumhuran

The beach east of the town glinted with a kaleidoscope of brightly coloured shells of every shape and curious design, crunching underfoot as I wandered along. Hosts of tiny crabs rushed helter-skelter into the surf. It was during the Dhofar Rebellion of the '60s and '70s against the British-supported Sultanate of Muscat and Oman. The sea was now the only source of food for the people of Mirbat. The Indian Ocean had made their great-grandfathers wealthy beyond their dreams for the monsoon winds had blown their slave ships in a few days from Zanzibar to Sur and thence to the Persian Gulf markets.

There were no others about on the Mirbat beach. I bathed at the edge of the surf, for the smell of my clothes was unpleasant. I searched them for fleas before putting them on again. The saltwater felt sticky, but my many bites stopped irritating.

We left Mirbat after three days and, at nightfall, came to the high cliffs of Kohr Rawhri and stopped to camp by the ruins of Sumhuran. Over 1,000 years ago it had been the greatest city of south-east Asia. I walked through these ruins of the Moon God's city and found the open mouth of a deep well above the sea cliffs. The place was eerie in the fleeting moonlight.

Sir Ranulph Fiennes
Explorer and author

Another time, when the mists withdrew for a while from the coastline leaving it humid but cool, the Colonel decided the few British and Indian officers in Umm al Ghawarif should spend one *jumma,* the Muslim day of rest, having a picnic on the white sands of Sumhuran. Three of my Land Rovers provided an escort through Taqa and the hills beyond to the cliffs where the ruins stood above the beach.

The Colonel produced an amazing supply of delicacies and wine from some portable freeze-boxes. The picnic was laid out on a rug over the velvet sand. The sea burst in explosive release, whipped up by the same winds that lashed the Somali horn, and swimming was not advisable.

Over to the west, beyond the pure white sand and the clutter of pink-bodied picnickers, the sea cliffs split in two where the creek called Khor Rawri once joined the sea. Before rockfalls and silt blocked its mouth, it used to form a safe harbour for ships from the Red Sea, Mesopotamia and the Far East.

The picnic over, we returned along the coast road. A week later, with another officer, I removed a newly placed anti-tank mine from the same road a mile from Taqah. The guerilla watchdogs had doubtless reported on the picnic and were hoping for another. ●

A traditional kotiya dhow
sailing off Mirbat on the
Dhofari coast of Oman

Freighter across the Bay of Bengal

My most treasured sea journey was not the most romantic, nor the most comfortable. I was filming *Around the World in 80 Days* and, owing to a series of misfortunes, my journey across the Bay of Bengal was in a battered old freighter with a Yugoslav crew. There was only room on the boat for the cameraman and myself, and as the rest of the crew flew on to Singapore, I was filmed swabbing decks, drinking Zlatorog beer and conducting inaudible interviews down in the engine room. When I was off-duty I stepped gingerly over the cargo, settled myself in the bows and watched the dolphins as they led us eastwards through a crystal clear sea. I've loved freighters ever since. ●

Michael Palin CBE
Comedian, actor and TV presenter

Fishermen pull in their daily catch on Silver Beach along the Bay of Bengal

Michael Palin photo: John Swannell

Motoring through the canals of Brunei

The capital of Brunei, Bandar Seri Begawan, is a cross between Disneyworld and something out of Somerset Maugham. In one direction sprawls a vast modern gold-domed mosque surrounded by skyscrapers with neon advertisements for international brand names. But across the harbour lies the old town, a settlement of simple wooden houses rising precariously out of the water on stilts. I had a spare afternoon so I went down to the waterfront.

A man with a motorboat offered to give me a tour. I got in. The Bruneians are a docile, sweet-natured people slightly bemused by the huge oil wealth that has transformed their simple society. As my driver gunned the motor, however, a demented grin spread over his face. We shot across to the old town, then, far from slowing as we reached the narrow canals separating the houses, he accelerated even more rapidly. Women and children cried out in fear. Multi-coloured lines of washing were left strewn in our wake. At the point when we seemed to be heading straight for a concrete post set in the water, I think I screamed. He swerved at the last moment. "You American," he said as I disembarked. "Like go fast."

"I'm English," I murmured weakly. In Bandar Seri Begawan one thing you'll never find is a strong drink. ●

Philip Hook
Senior director of
Sotheby's and author

The water village in Bandar Seri Begawan floats around the Sultan Omar Ali Saifuddin Mosque

Lord Jim

The Patna was a local steamer as old as the hills, lean like a greyhound, and eaten up with rust worse than a condemned water-tank. She was owned by a Chinaman, chartered by an Arab, and commanded by a sort of renegade New South Wales German, very anxious to curse publicly his native country, but who, apparently on the strength of Bismarck's victorious policy, brutalised all those he was not afraid of, and wore a 'blood-and-iron' air, combined with a purple nose and a red moustache. After she had been painted outside and whitewashed inside, eight hundred pilgrims (more or less) were driven on board of her as she lay with steam up alongside a wooden jetty.

They streamed aboard over three gangways, they streamed in urged by faith and the hope of paradise, they streamed in with a continuous tramp and shuffle of bare feet, without a word, a murmur, or a look back; and when clear of confining rails spread on all sides over

Joseph Conrad
(1857-1924)

the deck, flowed forward and aft, overflowed down the yawning hatchways, filled the inner recesses of the ship – like water filling a cistern, like water flowing into crevices and crannies, like water rising silently even with the rim. Eight hundred men and women with faith and hopes, with affections and memories, they had collected there, coming from north and south and from the outskirts of the East, after treading the jungle paths, descending the rivers, coasting in praus along the shallows, crossing in small canoes from island to island, passing through suffering, meeting strange sights, beset by strange fears, upheld by one desire. They came from solitary huts in the wilderness, from populous campongs, from villages by the sea. At the call of an idea they had left their forests, their clearings, the protection of their rulers, their prosperity, their poverty, the surroundings of their youth and the graves of their fathers. They came covered with dust, with sweat, with grime, with rags – the strong

men at the head of family parties, the lean old men pressing forward without hope of return; young boys with fearless eyes glancing curiously, shy little girls with tumbled long hair; the timid women muffled up and clasping to their breasts, wrapped in loose ends of soiled head-cloths, their sleeping babies, the unconscious pilgrims of an exacting belief.

"Look at dese cattle," said the German skipper to his new chief mate. An Arab, the leader of that pious voyage, came last. He walked slowly aboard, handsome and grave in his white gown and large turban. A string of servants followed, loaded with his luggage; the Patna cast off and backed away from the wharf. She was headed between two small islets, crossed obliquely the anchoring-ground of sailing-ships, swung through half a circle in the shadow of a hill, then ranged close to a ledge of foaming reefs. The Arab, standing up aft, recited aloud the prayer of travellers by sea. He invoked the favour of the Most High upon that journey, implored His blessing on men's toil and on the secret purposes of their hearts; the steamer pounded in the dusk the calm water of the Strait; and far astern of the pilgrim ship a screw-pile lighthouse, planted by unbelievers on a treacherous shoal, seemed to wink at her its eye of flame, as if in derision of her errand of faith.

She cleared the Strait, crossed the bay, continued on her way through the 'One-degree' passage. She held on straight for the Red Sea under a serene sky, under a sky scorching and unclouded, enveloped in a fulgor of sunshine that killed all thought, oppressed the heart, withered all impulses of strength and energy. And under the sinister splendour of that sky the sea, blue and profound, remained still, without a stir, without a ripple, without a wrinkle – viscous, stagnant, dead. The Patna, with a slight hiss, passed over that plain, luminous and smooth, unrolled a black ribbon of smoke across the sky, left behind her on the water a white ribbon of foam that vanished at once, like the phantom of a track drawn upon a lifeless sea by the phantom of a steamer. ●

North & Central America

A land of lush green waterways, dazzling cities, mountainous peninsulas, alpine lakes, rolling vineyards, chiselled peaks, and barren deserts

View across the Burrard Inlet waterfront in Vancouver to Canada Place, with its distinctive white sail design

By ship to Montreal

M y mother, my sister and I boarded the Empress of Australia in Liverpool docks, bound for Montreal, and then on by train to join my father in the middle of the prairies in the spring of 1954. Owned by the Canadian Pacific Railways, the Empress had been launched in 1924. Although I have dim memories of pale oak panelling and sweeping staircases, my sister and I were too busy washing our teddies' clothes and hanging them in the porthole to dry to pay much attention to the art deco all around us, let alone to the man permanently playing a grand piano at the foot of the sweeping staircase. (I was 12 at the time but, being timid and shortsighted, I still preferred teddies to football, air-guns, stamp albums and other manly pursuits.)

As we rounded the Giant's Causeway and headed into the Atlantic, the wind got up and the boat began to toss from side to side. For a brief moment we were hugely excited by it all, but then were both violently sick, and lay in our bunks to recover.

I remember very little about the six-day voyage apart from running round and round the deck – no doubt to the irritation of those hardy travellers braving the spray, the wind and the black flecks belched out by the ship's two yellow funnels – and wrapped in thick tartan rugs,

Jeremy Lewis
Writer, commissioning editor of *The Oldie*, and editor-at-large of the *Literary Review*

sat in deck-chairs reading detective stories by Margery Allingham or grappling with crossword puzzles. But I did acquire a lifelong passion for eating large meals on board ship, marvelling at the way in which the chairs were bolted to the floor and at the low wooden wall, which ran round the tables to prevent cutlery and crockery falling into our laps during a storm. My mouth still waters at the memory of such transatlantic treats as iced water, canned orange juice, waffles and maple syrup, none of them familiar items in post-war London. One day we were summoned on deck mid-meal to inspect an iceberg, dimly discerned through the mist on the starboard side.

One of the great pleasures of a sea voyage is the sense of being in limbo, far removed from the worries of everyday life. My worries were restricted to cutting my teddy's hair and wondering why it didn't grow back, and after a few days at sea a degree of boredom set in. It was a relief to find ourselves chugging down the Saint Lawrence River, and to pick out russet-coloured clapboard houses and white wooden churches on the steep green banks of the river. At Quebec I set foot on foreign soil for the first time in my life. Two days later we boarded a Canadian Pacific Railway train heading for Winnipeg and points west, also – as I soon discovered – heavily laden with waffles and maple syrup. ●

Percé Rock on the tip of the
Gaspé Peninsula in Quebec, Canada

Vancouver by cargo boat

My family travelled to Vancouver in Canada when I was 12, and in rather a novel way. In 1956 we, with a few other passengers, boarded a Dutch cargo boat in London's Royal Docks and set off on our journey to cross the Atlantic to the Panama Canal.

Our first port of call was the Azores, where we didn't disembark but gazed from our anchorage offshore at these extraordinary tree-clad islands rising steeply from the sea, populated with small towns and white houses. The journey to Vancouver took six weeks across a calm and vast Atlantic, where we saw shoals of flying fish, watched the porpoises racing ahead of the prow day after day, crossed the 'Wide Sargasso Sea' and on. Day after day there was nothing but the great and distant horizon, the sparkling water and the immense arc of glistening stars at night.

Travelling through the Windward Islands some whales joined us and blew great spouts of steam and water, almost within touching distance. Majestic, calm and graceful, they followed us past islands covered

Anna Ford
Journalist, TV presenter and newsreader

with palm trees, from where we smelt the strange and beguiling smells of foreign lands for the first time. We docked at Colón to take on oranges and exchange cargoes, and on through the Panama Canal and its locks where multi-coloured parrots flew screeching overhead and a bright green grasshopper the size of a hand landed on board.

After Panama and into the Pacific we hit a spectacular thunderstorm and the sky was black. Cruising up the coast of Mexico we left land far to our right, as the coast is notorious for wrecks and our old ship, SS Duivendijk (built in 1930), was on her last voyage. We stopped at Fisherman's Wharf in San Francisco, with its pungent smell of leather tanneries and the constant din of gantry cranes loading and unloading mixed with the cries and shouts of dozens of stevedores. On to Seattle before crossing to Vancouver Island, and then to Vancouver where, arriving in the evening I remember the bay of this great city with far twinkling lights, distant noises and the strange smells of the cargo docks. It was the journey of a lifetime and left me with a love of the sea and boat voyages. ●

Skyscrapers line the luxurious Coal Harbour waterfront in Vancouver

Portsmouth to the West Indies

For my National Service I was always determined to join the Navy. For four years on field days in my school's Cadet Corps I had dragged myself through the sodden expanses of Windsor Great Park on November afternoons, and I couldn't face any more of it. So the Navy it was, and after six months' training as a writer – only writers, stokers and cooks were available choices, the Seamanship branch taking too long to train – I found myself sitting at Chatham in June 1948, wondering what was to become of me. Most of us, as I well knew, would never be lucky enough to find a seagoing ship.

But I was. HMS Cleopatra was refitting in dry dock at Portsmouth, but in three months' time would be sailing on the Home Fleet Cruise to the West Indies. Imagine the excitement for an 18-year-old – his first visit to the

John Julius Norwich
History and travel
writer, TV and radio
presenter

tropics: the coconuts, the palm-fringed beaches, the calypsos… I couldn't wait. And the journey out was a joy, with the increasing warmth of every day that passed. The Home Fleet was some 30-strong in those days, and we took our time. It was 16 days before we reached Trinidad, our first stop. During the last ten days the entire Fleet stopped at four o'clock for swimming; over the side we went, and I remember the wonderful feeling of swimming in deliciously warm water some 15 or 20 miles deep. Only one mishap – when some young seaman dived straight into a Portuguese Man-of-War, amongst the most poisonous creatures in the sea. He recovered, but I can still hear the scream.

From Trinidad, it got better and better. The rum, inevitably, took its toll, but those next three weeks were among the most purely enjoyable of my life. I am delighted to relive them after more than 60 years. ●

*Orange sunset over a palm
beach in the West Indies*

John Julius Norwich photo: Camilla Panufnik

By liner to New York

During 1947 I went to New York to stay with friends of my parents. I travelled on the Queen Elizabeth, and returned after a month or so on the Queen Mary. The voyages were most exciting on those magnificent ships. There were so many stewards to look after your every wish, porters to carry your trunk, and dinner was always black tie.

I think the trip took five days, and I had to have a different evening dress for every night. It was really the most glamorous time. My Dad had provided me with a first class ticket. He felt that I had missed out on travel because of the war and wanted to make up for it. I stayed with friends in Connecticut, travelled to the Thousand Islands in the Saint Lawrence River, saw shows in New York, and listened to jazz in Harlem.

Some of the friends I stayed with, Bill and Ione Snodgrass, had just received a chest freezer. They were new at the time and I helped Ione to wrap endless joints of meat. (I still wonder if she used them all!) I went with her to New York to a radio show and she pushed me forward to join in singing *Take Me Out to the Ball Game*, a fairly simple song – and I won a Polaroid camera. It was a wonderful trip, and I doubt if I shall ever see the like again. ●

June Whitfield CBE
Actress

The QEII arrives in New York in her glory days on the high seas

Cruising the Caribbean

Following a successful five-day sail on the QE2 to New York to pick up our son and his backpack from the ritual trip to the Far East, my husband and I decided to celebrate our silver wedding anniversary with a cruise from Florida around the Caribbean.

Look. Cruising is what you make of it. There's a touch too much queuing, too many thumping great liners in dock, and you can't go swinging too many cats round in your cabin. Still, you can work out, be massaged, gamble, play bridge, shop 'til you drop anchor, or just sit and watch all human life just waddle past. Would I go again? Certainly I would although, perhaps, to a different location. The cruise staff were enchanting. Although I must say I jumped when I heard one of them say, "I dealing with the Jews". It took a moment before I realised he meant freshly squeezed grapefruit, orange or pineapple. When hundreds of Indonesian table crew filed out carrying flaming baked Alaskas on our last night, then stood to sing their national anthem, my eyes filled up again, and I realised I'm just a sucker for, as my dad would have said, the whole *mishegas*.

Back on dry land, the laborious transfer from boat to coach to hotel with luggage was almost enough to make me eat my words – but thanks to ten days' cruising I was too chunky to eat anything. ●

Maureen Lipman CBE
Actress and columnist

A cruise ship docks at the port of St George's, Grenada

Moby Dick

Some years ago – never mind how long precisely – having little or no money in my purse, and nothing particular to interest me onshore, I thought I would sail about a little and see the watery part of the world. It is a way I have of driving off the spleen and regulating the circulation. Whenever I find myself growing grim about the mouth; whenever it is a damp, drizzly November in my soul; whenever I find myself involuntarily pausing before coffin warehouses, and bringing up the rear of every funeral I meet; and especially whenever my hypos get such an upper hand of me that it requires a strong moral principle to prevent me from deliberately stepping into the street and methodically knocking people's hats off – then, I

Herman Melville
(1819-1891)

account it high time to get to sea as soon as I can. This is my substitute for pistol and ball. With a philosophical flourish Cato throws himself upon his sword; I quietly take to the ship. There is nothing surprising in this. If they but knew it, almost all men in their degree, some time or other, cherish very nearly the same feelings towards the ocean with me.

There now is your insular city of the Manhattoes, belted round by wharves as Indian isles by coral reefs – commerce surrounds it with her surf. Right and left, the streets take you waterward. Its extreme downtown is the battery, where that noble mole is washed by waves, and cooled by breezes, which a few hours previous were out of sight of land. Look at the crowds of water-gazers there.

Circumambulate the city of a dreamy Sabbath afternoon. Go from Corlears Hook to Coenties Slip, and from thence, by Whitehall, northward. What do you see? Posted like silent sentinels all around the town, stand thousands upon thousands of mortal men fixed in ocean reveries. Some leaning against the spiles; some seated upon the pier-heads; some looking over the bulwarks of ships from China; some high aloft in the rigging, as if striving to get a still better seaward peep. But these are all landsmen; of week days pent up in lath and plaster – tied to counters, nailed to benches, clinched to desks. How then is this? Are the green fields gone? What do they here?

But look! Here come more crowds, pacing straight for the water, and seemingly bound for a dive. Strange!

Nothing will content them but the extremest limit of the land; loitering under the shady lee of yonder warehouses will not suffice. No. They must get just as nigh the water as they possibly can without falling in. And there they stand – miles of them – leagues. Inlanders all, they come from lanes and alleys, streets and avenues – north, east, south, and west. Yet here they all unite. Tell me, does the magnetic virtue of the needles of the compasses of all those ships attract them thither?

Once more. Say you are in the country; in some high land of lakes. Take almost any path you please, and ten to one it carries you down in a dale, and leaves you there by a pool in the stream. There is magic in it. Let the most absent-minded of men be plunged in his deepest reveries – stand that man on his legs, set his feet a-going, and he will infallibly lead you to water, if water there be in all that region. Should you ever be athirst in the great American desert, try this experiment, if your caravan happen to be supplied with a metaphysical professor. Yes, as every one knows, meditation and water are wedded for ever.

But here is an artist. He desires to paint you the dreamiest, shadiest, quietest, most enchanting bit of romantic landscape in all the valley of the Saco. What is the chief element he employs? There stand his trees, each with a hollow trunk, as if a hermit and a crucifix were within; and here sleeps his meadow, and there sleep his cattle; and up from yonder cottage goes a sleepy smoke. Deep into distant woodlands winds a mazy way, reaching to overlapping spurs of mountains bathed in their hill-side blue. But though the picture lies thus tranced, and though this pine-tree shakes down its sighs like leaves upon this shepherd's head, yet all were vain, unless the shepherd's eye were fixed upon the magic stream before him. Go visit the Prairies in June, when for scores on scores of miles you wade knee-deep among Tiger-lilies – what is the one charm wanting? Water – there is not a drop of water there! Were Niagara but a cataract of sand, would you travel your thousand miles to see it?

Why did the poor poet of Tennessee, upon suddenly receiving two handfuls of silver, deliberate whether to buy him a coat, which he sadly needed, or invest his money in a pedestrian trip to Rockaway Beach? Why is almost every robust healthy boy with a robust healthy soul in him, at some time or other crazy to go to sea? Why upon your first voyage as a passenger, did you yourself feel such a mystical vibration, when first told that you and your ship were now out of sight of land? Why did the old Persians hold the sea holy? Why did the Greeks give it a separate deity, and own brother of Jove?

Surely all this is not without meaning. And still deeper the meaning of that story of Narcissus, who because he could not grasp the tormenting, mild image he saw in the fountain, plunged into it and was drowned. But that same image, we ourselves see in all rivers and oceans. It is the image of the ungraspable phantom of life; and this is the key to it all. ●

South America

Continent of tropical rainforests and toothy-edged mountain ranges, soaring waterfalls
and breathtaking gorges, white sand archipelagos and multicoloured sandstone cliffs

The spectacular waterfalls of the
Iguazú National Park, in the north
of Argentina's Misiones province

Tierra del Fuego Chile

t was the getting there that lit life up. It was October 2008, after what had been a tough few weeks, and we were in the air from Santiago in Chile, south over the cinnamon-coloured Andes to Punta Arenas, at the tip of South America.

It's a charmingly tumbleweed place of brightly painted corrugated-iron buildings; from there we took a little twin-engined Otter to Puerto Williams, the southernmost town in the world; and from there by helicopter down the Darwin Sound past vast glaciers to a small fjord called Seno Pia.

This is Tierra del Fuego, a Wagnerian landscape, where we were filming part of a series on Charles Darwin's effect on the politics of today's world. We were dropped off on a small beach where we were hoping to rendezvous with a schooner, the Philos, and sail part of Darwin's route, just a couple of days' worth,

Andrew Marr
BBC presenter, columnist and author

in the Beagle. Nobody about. I sat down on the granite sand and stared at the ice-floes sculpted into Dali-esque shapes – the wind had made birds, grasping hands, anvils, whirling branches. I drew. (I always draw.) Then, suddenly, round a corner came the schooner, tiny against the mountains. We scrambled aboard with a leaky old rubber boat.

Through rainstorms and sunsets, extreme-blue skies and dark green water, we sailed and filmed and drank whisky and exchanged stories. We saw not a sign of human life anywhere – not another boat, not a soul or building on the occasional wooded coves. Just for a couple of days, brought together by the curious single purpose of making a film, we felt sliced off and cut adrift from the other six billion. Though dissolving glaciers were all around, this seemed like the beginning of the world, not its end. These were Narnia days; the best of times. ●

Sunset in Ushuaia – the capital of Tierra del Fuego, and the southernmost city in the world

Orinoco South America

The Amazon would be wonderful, I thought, but the Orinoco was better. It's narrower, so you get a real sense of what's happening along the banks. From time to time we saw a small settlement of two or three tiny shacks, little more than some poles lashed together. No sides, of course, because the heat is too great. We never saw people but we heard their calls, signalling along the shore as our cruise ship passed by. It must have seemed to them like a spacecraft. An expert on board explained all the different birds to look out for, but my eye wasn't quick enough to see very much. I preferred a lonely perch away from other passengers, trying to catch some fleeting sense of its brooding beauty. Dense green foliage, impenetrable but infinitely varied, small creeks running inland, the stillness under changing clouds. ●

Dame Joan Bakewell
Broadcaster,
author and columnist

*Dense foliage runs along
the Tigre River tributary
of the Orinoco, Venezuela*

The Sacred Lake of the Andes

was a traveller bewitched by my first sight of Lake Titicaca, over half a century ago. An immense inland sea in the high Andes, almost 4,000 metres above sea level, it straddles the border between Peru and Bolivia and is the highest commercially navigable lake in the world. But dry statistics cannot convey the majestic grandeur of this vast expanse of water, fringed by the shimmering peaks of the Cordillera Real (or Royal Cordillera) mountain range. It is a place of mystery and magic as well as beauty, enshrined in ancient myths and legends, and possessed of a strange telluric power. There is an Aymara myth that this was the original garden of Eden, from which sprang all human life. Local fable also has it that the Inca dynasty traced its supernatural origins from one of the lake's largest islands, the Island of the Sun. The Sun God, Viracocha, commanded his son and daughter, Manco Capac and Mama Ojllo, to go forth until they reached the place where the golden staff they carried would sink into the ground of its own accord. Thus was the city of Cuzco founded.

For me that first vision was the start of a love affair that has lasted the rest of my life; a dream that culminated, decades later, in the building of my home on the shores of the Sacred Lake; and the creation of my own garden of Eden, cascading down in terraces to the water's edge. The lake and the Andes never cease

Dame Margaret Anstee
Former Under-Secretary-General of the United Nations, and writer

to enthral me, as I have described in my book, *The House on the Sacred Lake (and other Bolivian Dreams and Nightmares):*

"Dawn over the Andes is a daily spectacular, dizzying the spirit, except during those few days and weeks when the rains come to drench the parched altiplano briefly in green. It is my favourite time of day. Every morning I get up at the first glimmer of light and draw back the curtains. The surface of the lake is still grey and cold as steel, and through the clumps of eucalyptus down by the beach I can make out the shadowy outlines of small fishing boats, their solitary occupants pulling in the nets laid the night before, huddled against the biting chill of every dawn throughout the year, the silence broken only by the creak of straining oars.

"The sun – the ancient god of the Aymaras and the Incas – announces his presence long before his actual appearance. First he illuminates the lesser deities, the achachila who live in the mountains, as a broad band of pale light across the eastern sky etches the jagged graph of the Cordillera in sharp relief on the far horizon. Each day the colours are subtly different, sometimes pale saffron, sometimes a warm apricot, sometimes the most delicate intermingled pink and turquoise hues. As the light gathers the lake too gains in luminosity, reflecting the rainbow colours that now suffuse the heavens.

A reed boat on the calm waters of Lake Titicaca in Puno, Peru

"Then, at last, this crescendo of colour reaches its zenith. The sun breasts its way over the mountaintops, flooding my bedroom with a river of gold, and climbs swiftly up the sky, eclipsing all its minor harbingers. The other colours fade, both sky and lake reassume their intense, cobalt blue and the mountains become again a shimmering silver palisade, an idyllic scene that, for me, is incomparable to any other place on earth.

"If dawn is my favourite time of day on the Lake, sunset comes a close second. At Villa Margarita I take tea in my bedroom, the balcony windows thrown open on mountains, sky and lake throughout the day now closed, for as the sun sinks lower, so does the temperature. Lit by a pale golden light from the west, the mountains play out their last dramatic performance of the day. As the western sky deepens into gold and then fiery red, silhouetting the dark shapes of far hills on the distant fringes of the Lago Mayor that are far away in Peru, so the reflected and shifting colours of the sunset play on the peaks and gullies of the Royal Cordillera. The show does not last long for we are in the zone of the tropics here and night falls fast. First the distant Illimani fades into the gathering dark and then, one by one, the jagged peaks that stretch one hundred miles or so to the tumbled mass of the Illampu merge into the penumbra in their turn. Alone, the imposing cone of Huayno Potosi (literally 'the young man from Potosi') flaunts the last rays of the dying sun, flushes deep rose and then pink and is finally consumed

as if by its own fires in an all-enveloping opalescent haze.

"Down below the waters of the lake that a few moments before had been a mirror image of the pyrotechnics in the sky have also lapsed into darkness, swallowing up the small fishing boats that are once more laying their nets for the night in the bay below. Just before the light finally fails it is the far edge of the lake that seems to define the eastern horizon, as if marking the end of the known world.

"There is still one more intense pleasure to savour before the day finally comes to an end. Every night, before retiring to bed, I stand for a while under the wide glass roof of the entrance porch of Villa Margarita. From there I have an untrammelled and sheltered view of the Andean sky, a huge dark vault studded with a myriad of brilliant stars and galaxies, precious gems sparkling in the clear and frosty air. And on those nights blessed with a full moon the Sacred Lake comes alive again with all its ineffable magic.

"The Aymaras for long ages past have had their own cosmography, reading the stars not only in order to predict the weather for their crops and their sowing and harvesting seasons, but also for portents of forthcoming cataclysmic events, natural and manmade. It is at moments like these that one feels oneself caught up in the unfathomable mysteries of this most beautiful and magical place, adrift from the cares of the rest of the world." ●

Village life on the floating islands of Lake Titicaca, home to the Uros tribe

Journey along the Amazon

Rivers do it for me. History is shaped by these water highways, and for present-day travellers there is the constant interest of riverside life. From a slow-moving boat we can observe small communities still dependent on the river for their needs, watch wildlife or birds in the early morning, or visit cities which grew wealthy from river trade. In 1969 I travelled down most of the navigable length of the mightiest river in the world, the Amazon, on a variety of cargo boats. It was a pivotal experience in my travelling life.

So long ago and I didn't have a camera; just memories. On the first stretch from Pucallpa in Peru, the jungle overhung the banks on either side. From time to time the trees had been cleared for a scattering of mud-and-thatch huts. We stopped at one of these Shipibo villages to offload sugar and flour. As the captain laid the gangway plank the women ran down to the riverbank with goods for sale: pottery, fruit, and even animals. One passenger bought an albino squirrel monkey: pure white with a crinkly pink face and pale blue eyes. Further downriver I strolled around a village while the captain negotiated for meat. The locals had seen few foreigners and stared at me wide-eyed. I remember a

Hilary Bradt MBE
Publisher, writer
and lecturer

timid little girl with her not-so-cuddly toy pressed to her chest: a stuffed bullfrog.

From Iquitos I took a smaller, more basic boat where the few passengers slept in hammocks. A corner of the deck was curtained off and a bucket provided for a shower. The one toilet was occupied by a hen, which was replaced later by turtles. Both ended up on the dinner table. The boat stopped at a sandy beach and all the passengers started digging for turtle eggs.

From Leticia, in Colombia, I took a ferry across the river to the Brazilian border town of Benjamin Constant where, after a few days' wait, I boarded a three-deck 'bird cage' passenger boat heading for Manaus. It also carried a cargo of brazil nuts. The river was broad and sluggish, but the Brazilian passengers animated and fun. They played music, gambled at cards, and chatted. I had not found it easy making the switch from Spanish to Portuguese but one family spoke English. They told me that they'd heard that an American spaceship was heading for the moon. As darkness fell with equatorial suddenness, we watched it rise above the rubber plantations and tall ceiba trees. No one spoke. Next day in Manaus, a town with roads that go nowhere and people who go nowhere except by river, we learned that the American astronauts had landed on the moon. ●

*Two Scarlet Macaws – the
quintessential Amazon bird*

The Voyage of the Beagle

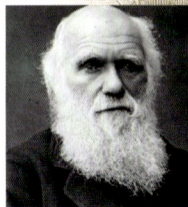

Charles Darwin
(1809-1882)

September 15th. This archipelago consists of ten principal islands, of which five exceed the others in size. They are situated under the Equator, and between five and six hundred miles westward of the coast of America. They are all formed of volcanic rocks; a few fragments of granite curiously glazed and altered by the heat can hardly be considered as an exception.

Some of the craters surmounting the larger islands are of immense size, and they rise to a height of between three and four thousand feet. Their flanks are studded by innumerable smaller orifices. I scarcely hesitate to affirm that there must be in the whole archipelago at least two thousand craters. These consist either of lava and scoriae, or of finely-stratified, sandstone-like tuff. Most of the latter are beautifully symmetrical; they owe their origin to eruptions of volcanic mud without any lava. It is a remarkable circumstance that every one of the twenty-eight tuff-craters which were examined had their southern sides either much lower than the other sides, or quite broken down and removed. As all these craters apparently have been formed when standing in the sea, and as the waves from the trade wind and the swell from the open Pacific here unite their forces on the southern coasts of all the islands, this singular uniformity in the broken state of the craters, composed of the soft and yielding tuff, is easily explained.

Considering that these islands are placed directly under the equator, the climate is far from being excessively hot; this seems chiefly caused by the singularly low temperature of the surrounding water, brought here by the great southern Polar current. Excepting during one short season very little rain falls, and even then it is irregular; but the clouds generally hang low. Hence, whilst the lower parts of the islands are very sterile, the upper parts, at a height of a thousand feet and upwards, possess a damp climate and a tolerably luxuriant vegetation. This is especially the case on the windward sides of the islands, which first receive and condense the moisture from the atmosphere.

In the morning (17th) we landed on Chatham Island, which, like the others, rises with a tame and rounded outline, broken here and there by scattered hillocks, the remains of former craters. Nothing could be less inviting than the first appearance. A broken field of black basaltic

lava, thrown into the most rugged waves, and crossed by great fissures, is everywhere covered by stunted, sunburnt brushwood, which shows little signs of life. The dry and parched surface, being heated by the noonday sun, gave to the air a close and sultry feeling, like that from a stove: we fancied even that the bushes smelt unpleasantly.

Although I diligently tried to collect as many plants as possible, I succeeded in getting very few; and such wretched-looking little weeds would have better become an arctic than an equatorial Flora. The brushwood appears, from a short distance, as leafless as our trees during winter; and it was some time before I discovered that not only almost every plant was now in full leaf, but that the greater number were in flower. The commonest bush is one of the *Euphorbiaceae*: an acacia and a great odd-looking cactus are the only trees which afford any shade. After the season of heavy rains, the islands are said to appear for a short time partially green. The volcanic island of Fernando Noronha, placed in many respects under nearly similar conditions, is the only other country where I have seen a vegetation at all like this of the Galapagos Islands.

The Beagle sailed round Chatham Island, and anchored in several bays. One night I slept on shore on a part of the island where black truncated cones were extraordinarily numerous: from one small eminence I counted sixty of them, all surmounted by craters more or less perfect. The greater number consisted merely of a ring of red scoriae or slags cemented together: and their height above the plain of lava was not more than from fifty to a hundred feet: none had been very lately active. The entire surface of this part of the island seems to have been permeated, like a sieve, by the subterranean vapours: here and there the lava, whilst soft, has been blown into great bubbles; and in other parts, the tops of caverns similarly formed have fallen in, leaving circular pits with steep sides. From the regular form of the many craters, they gave to the country an artificial appearance, which vividly reminded me of those parts of Staffordshire where the great iron-foundries are most numerous. The day was glowing hot, and scrambling over the rough surface and through intricate thickets was very fatiguing; but I was well repaid by the strange Cyclopean scene.

As I was walking along I met two large tortoises, each of which must have weighed at least two hundred pounds: one was eating a piece of cactus, and as I approached, it stared at me and slowly walked away; the other gave a deep hiss, and drew in its head. These huge reptiles, surrounded by the black lava, the leafless shrubs, and large cacti, seemed to my fancy like some antediluvian animals. The few dull-coloured birds cared no more for me than they did for the great tortoises. ●

A whale fluke in front of the snow-covered mountains of Paradise Bay, Antarctica

Toward the Poles

The vast wilderness and natural beauty of the Antarctic and Arctic Circles

Crossing the Drake Passage

C hasing seabirds is the best excuse ever devised for going to sea. And you can easily make the case for the British seaboard as the most enjoyable of all seabird habitats. But I'd say the more far-flung the better. The greatest excitement of all is the horrendous passage between Tierra del Fuego and the Antarctic Peninsula.

Once you poke your nose out beyond the Beagle Channel and head south across the Drake Passage, you face 600 miles of the most cantankerous seas on the planet. It's an oceanic gamble. In the foulest weather you hang on tight and hope to live till tomorrow. When it's just moderately lumpy you share the sea with great albatrosses and a plethora of petrels. On one of those miraculous calms you may see few birds but have a fin whale nudging alongside and keeping station for a companionable mile or two. Just once, there was a glassy sea swarming with dozens of them.

And then you reach the South Shetlands and a wonderland of icebergs and islands and beaches crowded with penguins. Greatest trip ever. ●

Tony Soper
Writer and broadcaster

A platoon of Chinstrap penguins explore King George Island, the largest of the South Shetland islands

Arctic adventures

When I was a child, in the 1950s, it was pretty rare for civilians to travel long distances on anything other than a liner, and my first trip was out to the Far East when I was five-and-a-half. In truth, I don't remember much about that, but I do remember the trip back very well. The captain had a chart where I could follow the progress of the ship on the way back, and certain sights have really stuck in my mind: seeing camels in Aden and the hanging gardens at Bombay (and no, I don't mean Babylon – everyone asks me that). We stopped at Pompei and Genoa, and were one of the last ships through Suez before the crisis shut the canal. There were lots of other children on board which was, of course, great fun – and we all loved not being at school.

More recently, I used to go cruising every year with my mother as she got more elderly, and did it into her 90s. She had always wanted to see the fjords, and I wanted to see the Arctic, so it was always cold water cruising. Warm water destinations don't much appeal to me, not least because of all the noise, the families. I prefer cruising with people of a certain age. We'd always have a cabin with a balcony, and would love sitting out

Ann Widdecombe
Former Shadow
Home Secretary,
author and columnist

on that, where we could see the world go by and not even have to go up on deck. Once we saw two tall ships sail over the horizon, and it felt like we'd travelled back in time. Another time we saw a polar bear: the captain stopped the ship, requested silence and after about an hour and a quarter the bear appeared. We all got to take pictures from the ship. Once, in the Arctic, we sailed through a gale-force storm; the ship crashed from side to side and all the water was sloshing out of the side of the pool, so I decided to go for a swim. Eventually another chap joined me, and we bounced around in there: I don't know if it was because it was a Norwegian ship, but no-one seemed very worried about the health and safety implications of what we were doing. I do, however, live in fear of a video of that surfacing one day.

I'm on a break from cruising at the moment – for now and for myself, I prefer more active holidays – but I'll definitely go back to it as I get older. Luckily, I've never been seasick in my life. The only similar thing I've done recently was a river cruise down the Danube, which was a very different experience. Of course, the boat was much smaller – it only carried around 120 passengers, as opposed to the 700 or so of many ocean-going ships which makes it more intimate, and allows you to get to know everyone so much better. ●

*A polar bear roams the ice sheets
in the cold blue Arctic light*

Yenisei River
by steamer

Water is the unconscious, said Jung. You do not dream innocently of dark or turbulent or even sunny water. Water always means something. Twelve years ago I travelled by steamer up Siberia's Yenisei River, going north into the Arctic Circle. Day after day the water became less a river than a whole sea on the move, as its banks grew more distant, less forested, less real. We seemed to be sliding over the edge of the world.

At one of the wretched villages where we berthed, a Polish priest embarked. For years, he said, he had been converting the Siberians along the river to the Catholic Melkite faith. He was barely five feet tall, and should have cut a derisory figure as he performed Mass for the passengers in the steamer's prow at evening. He processed back and forth in squelching trainers, and used an egg-cup as a symbolic chalice and dinged a fork against a tin in lieu of a bell. Yet he conducted himself like a god. I wondered what inspired him to travel for five years on the cold river, converting expatriate Germans and Siberian natives when he could. "These people are stupid," he said. "They have no culture at all. This land has had 70 years of Satan. And they drink."

Perhaps it was the river that hypnotised him, I thought, the mesmerising size of it, the sixth longest in the world. But one night he disembarked at a village in the dark, taking his enigma with him. ●

Colin Thubron CBE
Travel writer, novelist and President of the Royal Society of Literature

Panoramic view of the fjord surrounding Offersoy, a small village in the Arctic Circle

The Rime of the Ancient Mariner

And now the storm-blast came, and he
Was tyrannous and strong:
He struck with his o'ertaking wings,
And chased us south along.

With sloping masts and dipping prow,
As who pursued with yell and blow
Still treads the shadow of his foe,
And forward bends his head,
The ship drove fast, loud roared the blast,
And southward aye we fled.

And now there came both mist and snow,
And it grew wondrous cold:
And ice, mast-high, came floating by,
As green as emerald.

And through the drifts the snowy clifts
Did send a dismal sheen:
Nor shapes of men nor beasts we ken–
The ice was all between.

The ice was here, the ice was there,
The ice was all around:
It cracked and growled, and roared and howled,
Like noises in a swound! ●

Samuel Taylor
Coleridge
(1772–1834)

Rest of
the world

An incredible wealth of contrasts: harbour cities,
mountain backdrops, peaceful lakesides, deserted
beaches, remote desert and tropical rainforests

Sydney to Cape Town

Some years ago I completed one leg of a round-the-world yacht race from Sydney to Cape Town against the wind – it took five weeks. The average temperature was five degrees below freezing, and the average wind 50 knots. The maximum wave height reached 60 feet. On every one of the 14 yachts, someone had a nasty injury. On ours, one of the crew was thrown in the air and came down face-first onto a stanchion on deck, which smashed all his teeth and drew much blood. The yacht's doctor sewed him up, having first given him half a bottle of brandy by way of anaesthetic. It was actually a whole bottle, but the other half went on the floor. When the crewman eventually came reeling up on deck he had a terrible swollen lip. On catching sight of it, the rest of the crew burst into a spontaneous rendering of *Ol' Man River*.

Such is the reverence accorded to a shipmate after several weeks in the southern oceans. ●

HRH Prince Michael of Kent GCVO
Cousin to the Queen and grandson of King George V

A yacht regatta sails across Sydney Harbour, Australia

Shark encounter
Amirante Islands

We were coral-diving in the atolls of the Amirante Islands, west of the Seychelles, my son Stuart and I. My air tank gave out first, so I nudged him and pointed upwards. He gestured that I should go ahead, he had air to spare and wanted to continue cruising around the coral bommies scattered on the sandy shore.

I drifted up to the boat, handed over my tank but stayed in the water, with fins and mask still on, looking down 30 feet to my son. Then I saw the shark. Huge, drifting slowly through the coral towards the unsuspecting diver. What does a father do?

I submerged after one giant breath and finned frantically back down, pumping hard, using too much oxygen, desperate to warn him of the cruising monster. Finally, with no air left, I reached him, grabbed his arm and pointed. The shark came around the coral head.

Stuart, long a student of every shark in the sea, glanced, nodded, gave me a pitying look and made a cradling motion with his arms. A nurse shark, quite harmless. I rocketed back to the surface, risking the bends, to be hauled aboard by Creole arms, flapping like a beached plaice and making a vow. This is the last time I risk a heart attack for young smarty-pants. ●

Frederick Forsyth CBE
Author and columnist

Crystal clear waters off the beautiful island of St Pierre in the Seychelles

Swimming
with dolphins

Passions are best when shared, and I particularly enjoy sharing my passion for the sea with one particular group, dolphins. On small ship voyages you often see large schools or pods, moving at speed and leaping and diving with joyous abandon. Such is their attraction that everyone rushes to the ship's rail to catch sight of their spectacular dance.

Once I was in the Aegean on a small yacht when two dolphins came to join us and ride our bow wave; so close you could almost touch them, they appeared to glance up at us conspiratorially. They stayed on the wave for hours, simply enjoying the water and the movement. They are also ubiquitous, frequenting every corner of every ocean, while river dolphins inhabit the great waterways of Asia and South America. I have seen them in the South China Sea, in the warm Caribbean, off cold Scottish islands and even in the Suez Canal.

No wonder dolphins figure so prominently in the myths of so many civilisations, from Minoan Crete to Polynesia; yet every time I venture into the water, armed with snorkelling gear and flippers, I am reminded that I am indeed a land-locked mammal whose movements cannot be compared with the superb aquatic athleticism of the dolphins. ●

Dr Alan Borg CBE
Former Director of the Victoria & Albert Museum, Librarian of the Venerable Order of St John, and Vice-President of the Foundling Museum

Sailing off the north west coast of Morocco with dolphins playing at the bow

The deep blue sea

From childhood, the sight of light on water has always been special for me. It has brought me the purest pleasure, only equalled by that of a smile on a child's face, preferably those of my own children. Light on water has its own flow, born of the water but moving on its own, alike but different to light on the eye. So, travel to places with water – its mass and flow, colour and depth – has always fascinated me.

Childhood brought cruises in the Mediterranean and along the Norwegian coast, but what a greater joy to be an adult and to see great seas for the first time, to visit the wondrous harbours of the Pacific – San Francisco or Manila, Vancouver or Hong Kong – and watch a sunset slip like a yolk into the dark of the ocean off Borneo,

Jeremy Black MBE
Historian, author
and Professor
of History at the
University of Exeter

or to revisit cities such as Lyon and Budapest from the river. Sailing away from Budapest is totally different to leaving it by rail.

I like swimming in waters I have never before visited. Going into the sea off Carmel and realising, after a while, that I was not alone in the Pacific was a moment of total surprise. I reached the surface to discover a seal as big as a man on one side looking at me, with another on the other side and a third behind, all under a clear California sky. Being on the deck of the USS Missouri in the harbour of Peal Harbor giving a lecture on 'Why the Allies Won World War II' was very moving too.

Wherever it is, water can be both exhilarating and will bring moments of joy and also periods of relaxation to an over-busy life. ●

*A school of barracuda in the blue
waters off Queensland, Australia*

Pumping water in Malawi

When *The Times* sent me to Malawi to write about a water-aid charity for their Christmas appeal, I was expecting a pleasant sojourn in a warm country where I'd write a couple of helpful columns – and learn not very much. People need water, I figured, so you help them dig a well and pump it out – end of story.

Instead, accompanied by a band of stalwarts from Pump Aid, I had my misconceptions blown away.

'People need water'. Well, obviously; but people aren't stupid. Bits of the African continent are cruelly dry, but not most of it. Most Africans have already got water of a sort, or they'd have died or gone somewhere else. Peasant farmers are better at digging than Western students on a gap year, and Africans have been digging

Matthew Parris
Journalist, travel writer and former MP

wells since time immemorial.

It's not the presence of a supply, I learned, but the clean, secure accessing of the supply. That means installing a pump so you can seal the well against flies, animals, dirt and light. Rural Africans don't need to be told this – but the classic lever pump is an expensive and fairly temperamental beast, hard to repair or service without engineering. The Elephant Pump was just such an invention: a pump that required nothing but a bit of PVC pipe, a rope with some rubber washers tied into it, a wheel and a crank. Assemble the materials and the villagers did all the rest with mud bricks.

It was cheap, it was simple, it put the ball back into the villagers' court, and – once you got the hang – it was obvious. What was needed, I discovered, wasn't always billions of aid money, but often a network of dedicated teams, a small material contribution, and a big idea. ●

Over 1.1 billion people in the world do not have access to clean, safe water

Twenty Thousand Leagues Under the Sea

O n January 13, arriving in the Timor Sea, Captain Nemo raised the island of that name at longitude 122°. This island, whose surface area measures 1,625 square leagues, is governed by rajahs. These aristocrats deem themselves the sons of crocodiles, in other words, descendants with the most exalted origins to which a human being can lay claim. Accordingly, their scaly ancestors infest the island's rivers and are the subjects of special veneration. They are sheltered, nurtured, flattered, pampered, and offered a ritual diet of nubile maidens; and woe to the foreigner who lifts a finger against these sacred saurians.

But the Nautilus wanted nothing to do with these nasty animals. Timor Island was visible for barely an instant at noon while the chief officer determined his position. I also caught only a glimpse of little Roti Island, part of this same group, whose women have a well-established reputation for beauty in the Malaysian marketplace.

After our position fix, the Nautilus's latitude bearings were modulated to the southwest. Our prow pointed to the Indian Ocean. Where would Captain Nemo's fancies take us? Would he head up to the shores of Asia? Would he pull nearer to the beaches of Europe? Unlikely choices for a man who avoided populated areas! So would he go down south? Would he double the Cape of Good Hope, then Cape Horn, and push on to the

Jules Verne
(1828-1905)

Antarctic pole? Finally, would he return to the seas of the Pacific, where his Nautilus could navigate freely and easily? Time would tell.

After cruising along the Cartier, Hibernia, Seringapatam, and Scott reefs, the solid element's last exertions against the liquid element, we were beyond all sight of shore by January 14. The Nautilus slowed down in an odd manner, and very unpredictable in its ways, it sometimes swam in the midst of the waters, sometimes drifted on their surface.

During this phase of our voyage, Captain Nemo conducted interesting experiments on the different temperatures in various strata of the sea. Under ordinary conditions, such readings are obtained using some pretty complicated instruments whose findings are dubious to say the least, whether they're thermometric sounding lines, whose glass often shatters under the water's pressure, or those devices based on the varying

resistance of metals to electric currents. The results so obtained can't be adequately double-checked. By contrast, Captain Nemo would seek the sea's temperature by going himself into its depths, and when he placed his thermometer in contact with the various layers of liquid, he found the sought-for degree immediately and with certainty.

And so, by loading up its ballast tanks, or by sinking obliquely with its slanting fins, the Nautilus successively reached depths of 3,000, 4,000, 5,000, 7,000, 9,000, and 10,000 meters, and the ultimate conclusion from these experiments was that, in all latitudes, the sea had a permanent temperature of 4.5° centigrade at a depth of 1,000 meters.

I watched these experiments with the most intense fascination. Captain Nemo brought a real passion to them. I often wondered why he took these observations. Were they for the benefit of his fellow man? It was unlikely, because sooner or later his work would perish with him in some unknown sea! Unless he intended the results of his experiments for me. But that meant this strange voyage of mine would come to an end, and no such end was in sight.

Be that as it may, Captain Nemo also introduced me to the different data he had obtained on the relative densities of the water in our globe's chief seas. From this news I derived some personal enlightenment having nothing to do with science.

It happened the morning of January 15. The captain, with whom I was strolling on the platform, asked me if I knew how salt water differs in density from sea to sea. I said no, adding that there was a lack of rigorous scientific observations on this subject.

"I've taken such observations," he told me, "and I can vouch for their reliability."

"Fine," I replied, "but the Nautilus lives in a separate world, and the secrets of its scientists don't make their way ashore."

"You're right, Professor," he told me after a few moments of silence. "This is a separate world. It's as alien to the earth as the planets accompanying our globe around the sun, and we'll never become familiar with the work of scientists on Saturn or Jupiter. But since fate has linked our two lives, I can reveal the results of my observations to you."

"I'm all attention, Captain."

"You're aware, Professor, that salt water is denser than fresh water, but this density isn't uniform. In essence, if I represent the density of fresh water by 1.000, then I find 1.028 for the waters of the Atlantic, 1.026 for the waters of the Pacific, 1.030 for the waters of the Mediterranean..."

Aha, I thought, so he ventures into the Mediterranean?

"...1.018 for the waters of the Ionian Sea, and 1.029 for the waters of the Adriatic."

Assuredly, the Nautilus didn't avoid the heavily travelled seas of Europe, and from this insight I concluded that the ship would take us back – perhaps very soon – to more civilized shores. I expected Ned Land to greet this news with unfeigned satisfaction.

For several days our work hours were spent in all sorts of experiments, on the degree of salinity in waters of different depths or on their electric properties, coloration, and transparency, and in every instance Captain Nemo displayed an ingenuity equalled only by his graciousness toward me. Then I saw no more of him for some days and again lived on board in seclusion. ●

Introducing
Noble Caledonia

A select cruise operator for seasoned travellers, offering unique travel experiences to the far flung corners of the world

Noble Caledonia opens the doors to incredible journeys across the world. Since our establishment in 1991, we have made it our aim to offer clients unique experiences with like-minded travellers – whether you are one of 100 aboard an exploration cruise of Antarctica, or one of 15 exploring the historic route of Tamerlane.

We continue to expand our repertoire to include new and unusual destinations shaped by world events, discoveries and extraordinary human endeavours. Our range of trips includes sea cruises, river cruises, escorted tours, train journeys or combinations of any of these – each one promising to take you on an unforgettable adventure. ●

Contents

The story so far

There's turmoil in the Middle East and recession hitting the UK, and even the most intrepid travellers are starting to feel a little wary about international travel... It all sounds rather familiar, doesn't it? But this isn't today; rather, it's back in 1991 when Noble Caledonia was established.

It all started with Andrew Cochrane, then a travel industry marketing expert of some considerable experience, who made a call to Christer Salén, Swedish owner of a small ship called Caledonian Star. A plan was set in motion to improve the way the ship was marketed, and from this point onward things snowballed quite quickly. First, a new company was created to market the Caledonian Star, and given a name – Noble Caledonia. Within two weeks, an office was set up in Mayfair, stationery was printed, and the first advert was placed in *The Daily Telegraph* – Noble Caledonia was on its way.

Happily, the first Caledonian Star cruise – to West Africa in 1991 – was a success. Since then, we have steadily grown our offering of tours and cruises, responding to wishes and ideas from our regular clients and searching out the new, exciting and unusual at all times. Our aim is always to provide a unique, interesting and educational travel experience; a holiday, yes, but always more than that too.

Whilst our repertoire has expanded over the years to include cruises by river and sea, and

NOBLE CALEDONIA TIMELINE

In the beginning...
Noble Caledonia is established, and we move into our original offices in Charles Street, Mayfair.

1991

'The little blue ship'
The Caledonian Star becomes our flagship vessel. Originally a fishing trawler, she could carry just over 100 passengers.

1991

Charity begins at home
We give the profits of our first Caledonian Star cruise – to West Africa – to the World Hunger Foundation after witnessing the suffering of some African communities visited en route.

1991

Discovering new territory
Noble Caledonia offers its first 'land tour' – a four-night break to Hong Kong.

1992

Making tracks to Russia
Noble Caledonia introduces the Bolshoi Express St Petersburg to Tashkent, our first holiday in which the principle transport is by private train.

2001

A very special river vessel
MS Johann Strauss becomes our river cruise flagship on the Danube, sailing from the North Sea to the Black Sea and back.

2001

Leading the way
MS Island Sky replaces the Caledonian Star as our flagship sea vessel.

2001

tours by coach, train, plane – or, often, some combination of all three – what has remained constant is our knowledge and expertise. Our staff, in the office and in the field, have grown with us, and their dedication and experience has helped to shape the high level of planning, quality and personalised service that has become our hallmark.

Twenty years on, there is still turmoil in the Middle East, and the world is in the midst of yet more economic uncertainty. However, Noble Caledonia goes from strength to strength. From our modest beginnings we have grown to the point where we're now generally recognised as being Britain's leading small ship cruise specialist, with a loyal following and an ever-developing portfolio of innovative and enticing tours and cruises.

Along the way, there have been changes: in 2006, the majority shareholding passed from Christer Salén to his daughter Katarina Salén and her husband, Per Magnus Sander; the Island Sky and her sister ship formerly known as the Hebridean Spirit have replaced the Caledonian Star as our flagships for sea cruising; and the Johann Strauss leads our portfolio of river cruises.

We have followed our vision, and our tours and cruises encompass wildlife, culture, history or music in the UK, Europe, the Far East, Central and South America, Australia and the Pacific, Africa, the Indian Ocean and even the Polar regions. One thing is certain though: a tour with Noble Caledonia will never be 'just a holiday'. ●

Onwards and upwards
Noble Caledonia outgrows its Mayfair offices, and relocates to our current base at Chester Close in Belgravia.

2001

Classical onboard entertainment
We celebrate Mozart's bicentenary with our biggest-ever musical enterprise, chartering eight vessels in conjunction with the London Festival Opera company.

2006

Family business
The current owners, Katarina Salén and her husband Per Magnus Sander, buy Noble Caledonia from her father, Christer Salén.

2006

Voyages of discovery
MS Island Sky undergoes an extensive refurbishment.

2010

Journeys down south
MS Island Sky heads south to explore South America and South Georgia. Read more about her on page 112.

2011

Exploring Europe's rivers
MS Johann Strauss is refurbished. Amongst her many varied itineraries there's often an emphasis on music and gardens; you can read more about her on page 113.

2011

Right from the start
Many of our staff, both in the office and in the field, have been with us since the beginning – and played an important role in our growth.

2011

MS Island Sky

With a high ratio of crew to passengers – she never carries more than 114 people, despite being large enough for many more – Island Sky is one of our best-loved ships. She combines a relaxing cruising experience with the excitement of the unusual destinations that she specialises in. Imagine the experience of a country hotel that moves from one thrilling, rarely visited location to another, and you'll have some idea of the unique adventure that Island Sky offers.

This is not a cruise ship for lovers of organised entertainment and deck games. Instead, Island Sky offers relaxed, no-pressure voyages of discovery with high quality service. Island Sky offers large outside decks and 57 spacious suites, some with private balconies, as well as such luxuries as a top-deck Jacuzzi, a pianist who plays in the bar periodically throughout the day, and even a small onboard hairdressing salon. ●

Our much-loved MS Island Sky is one of the finest small ships in the world, with unusually large suites and spacious decks

Built to the highest specifications, Johann Strauss is one of the biggest river-going cruise ships afloat today

MS Johann Strauss

The 90-cabin, four-star MS Johann Strauss redefines travel along Europe's most spectacular waterways, including the Danube and Rhine. Built in 2004 and refurbished in 2011, Johann Strauss boasts 60 cabins with wonderful French balconies. Although she can take up to 180 passengers, we never carry more than 160 for added comfort.

Passengers can enjoy excellent views through the floor-to-ceiling windows of the top-deck restaurant, lounge bar and café. Also, the ship is furnished with all the facilities of a well-equipped hotel – from a gym and sauna to a television and telephone in each cabin. We guarantee a friendly, informal atmosphere while travelling onboard Johann Strauss under the care of our highly experienced cruise directors, hotel staff and Captain. Well-organised and interesting excursions ashore are complemented by our expert guest speakers, who also provide informative and entertaining talks as you sail along. ●

Sailing into the *wilderness*

For a great chunk of the 20th century, the White Sea – a huge southern inlet on the Barents Sea, which runs along the north west coast of Russia – was a major Soviet naval and submarine base, and pretty much out of bounds for foreigners. Notably larger than Lake Superior, the largest of North America's Great Lakes, it has a relatively narrow entrance, four main bays, and is scattered with tiny islands.

Though beautiful, surrounded by mountains and dotted with tiny islands, the White Sea is little visited by foreigners, and retains a genuine sense of mystery. Noble Caledonia's recently introduced 14-day White Sea Odyssey cruise perfectly shows the benefits of small ship cruises – minor ports can be used, smaller inlets investigated, waters off the beaten track explored. Plus, the more manageable number of passengers onboard – MS Island Sky carries no more than 114 guests – allows a genuine sense of community to develop.

Though it begins at Edinburgh's port of Leith, the cruise is concentrated on the famous port of Archangel, and on the Solovetsky Islands where Stalin built one of his famous Gulags. A particular highlight is the 16th-century Solovetsky Monastery, a vast but perfectly preserved medieval fortress with a fascinating and turbulent history. ●

Dan Wikingson
Captain of the MS Island Sky, executive vice president of Salén Ship Management (SSM)

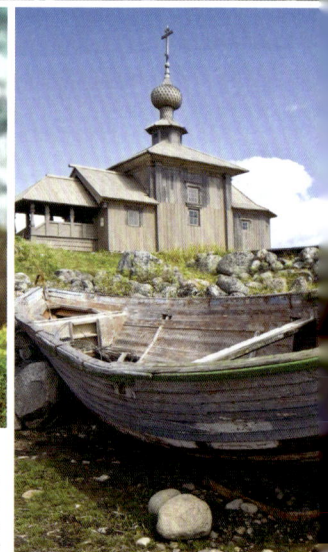

From the Solovetsky Monastery to Archangel, the White Sea Odyssey cruise uncovers the secrets of a once forbidden land

"It's as far away from a mass market tourist destination as you can get"

Captain Dan Wikingson, who took MS Island Sky on our first White Sea Odyssey cruise in 2011, outlines its unique delights…

Dan, this is a new cruise, isn't it?

It is certainly the first time it's been done in quite a while. We begin in Scotland but things start to get really exciting when we reach Bergen in Norway and go up through the fjords; the entire area up there is wonderful. Highlights would have to be Trollfjord and the North Cape, generally said to be Europe's most northerly point – beyond it there's only the North Pole. Up there you really feel you are in the wilderness.

Expedition cruises tend to be a very different experience to destination cruises, don't they?

Indeed! On the expedition cruises our passengers are prepared to suffer a bit to get to where they want to go. Typically, not many people have been where we're going, and there aren't many ports in these areas that will take even a ship as small as the Island Sky.

What are the advantages of small ship cruises?

You're in a fairly close environment, so it's brilliant for getting to know people and hearing all sorts of stories; our guests tend to be dedicated, seasoned travellers who've got tons of amazing experiences to talk about, so it's always a very interesting crowd to be with. It's a very different experience to the 3,000-guest Caribbean cruise ships, that's for sure.

And what are the challenges that you have to cope with when cruising?

The biggest one is, of course, the risk of rain, but in the summer the seas are kind and we were very lucky with the weather last year. Everyone says the old Solovetsky Monastery is particularly spectacular… it got to me completely! It has a very dramatic history, what with being a concentration camp at one time. It is now a fully-restored working monastery with monks of the Orthodox Church living there.

Part of the appeal is that I know I can't say to my wife, 'Shall we go to Solovetsky?' because there is no such trip; without the likes of Island Sky there's no real way for Westerners to get there. There's a certain amount of domestic tourism from Archangel, but even that's pretty limited, and there are no other international tourists. It's as far away from a mass market tourist destination as you can get, and I believe that most of the passengers feel something special when we get there. I had very high expectations of the White Sea and it turned out to be even better.

Where else would you like to travel?

With the opening up of Russia there's been talk about doing the entire Northern Sea Route, going along the top of Russia to the Pacific Ocean. It would take four or five weeks, but it would be amazing. In the meantime, the White Sea cruise has been a big hit – and I'm looking forward to doing a few more of those. ●

Life in the
slow lane

O ffering a completely different experience to ocean voyages, the river cruise has been a huge success for Noble Caledonia in recent years. Land is always within reach, you can visit a major world city every day of the cruise, and it offers a generally more comfortable experience for those of us with, let's say, more wobbly sea legs.

MS Johann Strauss is one of the largest craft currently working the big European waterways and her captain, Vasily Mariceanu, is hugely experienced on these rivers. Born in the Danube Delta region, he developed a strong relationship with his surroundings from an early age, so it wasn't surprising that after three years in the Navy he couldn't resist the "call of the Danube", where he has been sailing since 1978. His knowledge of the Danube, Rhine, Main and RMD Canal make him the ideal Captain for our itineraries, which stretch from the North Sea to the Black Sea. ●

Vasily Mariceanu
Captain of MS Johann Strauss since she was commissioned in 2004

Exploring the Danube valley, from Vienna to Budapest, with highlights including Melk Abbey and Bratislava Castle

"I love the River Danube the most… I find it endlessly fascinating with a strong personality"

Captain Vasily Mariceanu talks about exploring Europe by river cruise onboard MS Johann Strauss...

What makes MS Johann Strauss such a special river vessel?
The ship is 127m long and just over 11m wide, and it weighs 2,461 tonnes – that makes it about as big a ship as you can navigate on a river like the Danube. The most important dimensions are the height – 6.6m – and our 1.7m draft. These really come into play on the canals or minor rivers we travel down from the Rhine to the Danube; occasionally we have to take on ballast water so that we can just squeeze under bridges. One day I got it slightly wrong and the bridge knocked my hat off, but the ship still just cleared it!

Do you see a loyal following of customers on your cruises?
I love the Noble Caledonia customers! I'd be happy to sail with them for the rest of my life: every time I meet them for welcome cocktails I recognise a face or two, for we have a great many people who come back to us again and again for further holidays. We've been doing Noble Caledonia cruises for five seasons now, and it's turning into one big happy family.

Where do you travel on MS Johann Strauss?
We do many different cruises; the longest is from Amsterdam to the Black Sea and takes 23 days. I particularly love doing that one because it gives me time to meet all the passengers properly. Amsterdam-Budapest is a two-week cruise, as is Budapest-Black Sea; then we have the opera tour which is special because we have London opera experts onboard, which the passengers tend to love.

How does a river cruise differ to a sea cruise?
All day, and in the evening, the passengers have an ever-changing panorama to look at, whereas an ocean ship goes from harbour to harbour and in between there often aren't any mountains or little towns to look at. We have passengers who sit up on deck doing paintings, which is more rare to see at sea, plus we don't have storms or rough seas; it's quiet, so nobody gets afraid.

And what is the appeal of river cruising?
On the Rhine, people love the fact that around every bend there's another amazing castle to look at, while the Danube is slightly different; it's so big that people get fascinated by the river itself – such as how a river can be almost 3km wide and 75m deep in parts.

Which river cruise is your favourite?
Personally, I love the Danube the most; it is my home, my master, my god. I've been working on it for 32 years and find it endlessly fascinating with a strong personality; I respect and love it. My whole life has been spent on the Danube Delta; I first went fishing with my grandfather here when I was five years old – and I'm still here! ●

Cruise highlights

Holidays and journeys by land have their virtues. Noble Caledonia offers a range of land tours, including some very special private train journeys through Europe, Asia and Africa – but there's nothing quite like the experience of travelling by ship. You get to see places and wildlife that would otherwise be either virtually or completely inaccessible, and some sights are just best witnessed from the water.

Noble Caledonia cruises take in such rare experiences as whale-spotting in Norway and Argentina, and such unforgettable sights as calving glaciers at Lake Pehoe in Chile's Torres del Paine National Park – but here are some of our favourites... ●

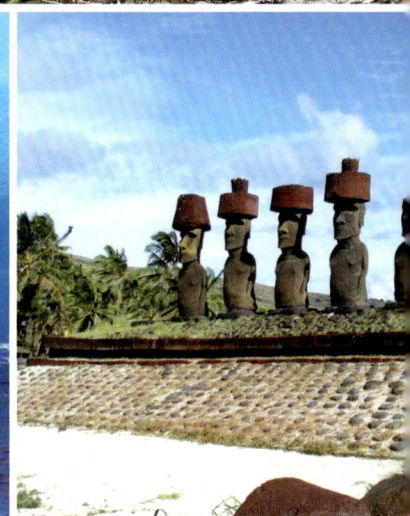

1
PENGUINS
ANTARCTICA
Our voyages to the Antarctic Peninsula are always full of unforgettable sights. It's hard to think of another place that combines the beautiful and the demanding with the ability to fire the imagination in quite such a way – but few can compete with the enormous tabular icebergs, covered in hundreds of huddling penguins. Antarctica remains a world apart, a majestic final frontier likely to surpass the most jaded traveller's expectations.

2
MILFORD SOUND
NEW ZEALAND
Coastal voyages around New Zealand offer access to an unpolluted landscape of remarkable natural beauty, from geysers and boiling mud to snow-capped mountains, rainforests and enchanting sandy bays. Most spectacular of all, though, are the steep-sided glacial fjords, including the incredible, waterfall-saturated Milford Sound in the South Island, called "the eighth Wonder of the World" by Rudyard Kipling.

3
MOAI
EASTER ISLAND
In the remote southeastern Pacific stands Easter Island, famous for its Moai monumental statues. Almost 900 statues dot the coast – giant heads and torsos carved from solidified volcanic ash and standing up to ten metres tall. With the heaviest of them weighing over 80 tons, their creation by Polynesian colonists around 700 years ago is nothing less than remarkable; the impression these enigmatic figures make is unforgettable.

4
BROWN BEAR
RUSSIAN FAR EAST
Our love of smaller cruise ships, rarely explored locations, and expeditions to shore using Zodiac inflatables allows us to glimpse the rarest of wildlife, often remarkably close at hand. One of the highlights of our tour of the 'Pacific Ring of Fire' – along Russia's volcanic, largely uninhabited Kamchatka Peninsula and isolated Kuril Islands – are up-close encounters with brown bear and red fox, rarely seen in their natural environment.

5
TRANSFIGURATION
CHURCH
KIZHI, RUSSIA
The island of Kizhi sits in the centre of Russia's Lake Onega, home to a vast open-air state museum. It contains over 80 historical wooden structures, the most famous of which is the Transfiguration Church, the oldest part of which dates back to the early 1700s. Difficult to get to other than by boat, the church is a remarkable sight, with a huge, lightly-decorated stack of 22 domes.

6
SWALLOW'S NEST
UKRAINE

Founded by the ancient Greeks, the popular Ukrainian port of Crimea on the Black Sea is full of spectacular architecture. One particularly unforgettable sight is the tiny but famous Lastochkino Gnezdo castle – known as the Swallow's Nest, or the 'Castle of Love'. Perched on Avrorianska rock, high above the sea, it was apparently built by a famous general to house a beautiful girl that he'd taken captive.

7
POLAR BEARS
ARCTIC

On the Svalbard (cold shores) archipelago, high in the Arctic Circle, the coming of summer opens up oft-frozen sea passages. This allows Noble Caledonia ships and Zodiacs to explore rarely visited bays on Spitsbergen and other islands – home to seals, foxes, reindeer, a host of seabirds and polar bears. A small ship tour is the only practical way to see these magnificent predators on their home ground.

8
MONT SAINT-MICHEL
FRANCE

About a kilometre off the coast of Normandy sits a rocky island, home to a castle-like monastery dating back to the 8th century. Most of the current building is from 400 years later – and used at various times as a prison and a fortress. The inspiration for the design of Minas Tirith in *The Lord of the Rings* films, it's one of those places where human construction and the natural world combine gloriously.

9
SAN BLAS ISLANDS
PANAMA

It's one of the most remarkable island chains we know: around 378 tiny 'stepping stones' and cays – only 49 of which are inhabited – lying to the east of the entrance to the Panama Canal. Many of them are barely above sea level and some are covered in buildings. They form part of a 'Hidden Caribbean', rarely visited by cruise ships, and known for their tribal inhabitants, and white sand beaches.

10
BLUE-FOOTED BOOBY
GALAPAGOS ISLANDS

With their bright-blue webbed feet and ingratiating waddle of a courtship dance, the Blue-footed Booby is native to Ecuador's Galapagos and a number of other tropical Pacific islands. It is one of the crowd-pleasing highlights of any visit to this largely unspoiled archipelago, inspiration to Charles Darwin and home of the giant tortoise, marine iguanas and many other species of exotic and colourful wildlife.

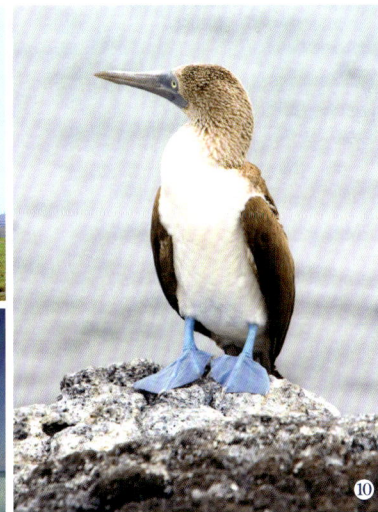

AN INSIDER'S STORY

Peter Warwick, a guest speaker on Noble Caledonia small ship cruises, shares his experiences of travelling along the world's inland waterways and rivers – and reveals his favourite destination by water...

"Arriving by water is a joy"

Peter Warwick
Chairman of Thames Alive, The 1805 Club, and the International Committee for Waterloo 200

We have all experienced arrival at the world's major airports. They attempt to be different, but we know the hassle is just the same. We could be anywhere. Arriving by water is a joy: it is leisurely, more in keeping with the human psyche, and each port is so very different. Maybe this explains the wave of popularity for luxury small ship cruising and themed itineraries; cruises where guests prefer to explore as they cruise into the autumn of their lives, rather than empty their wallets in the onboard shops and casinos of the 'giant, hideous hotel-liners'. Where the hotel is in the ship rather than the other way round; where the deck corridors do not ebb to a distant infinity; where the experience of the ship is the equivalent of adding another destination to the itinerary; and where the salt spray is forever close.

As one cruise veteran said: "These voyages are like a life's journey. There's something powerful about the way they separate you from reality and the world's troubles." Isn't that just what people like to do on holiday: to get away from it all! ●

*Clockwise, from top centre: Explore the world on
a Noble Caledonia small ship with sights including
the spectacular Amalfi Coast in Italy, the Big Almaty
Lake in Kazakhstan, the medieval town of Korcula
in Croatia, and the Karnak Temple in Luxor*

"Nothing like it"

Because I give lectures on small ship cruises, I consider myself the luckiest person in the vessel. I get to know the crew and the passengers (although I prefer them to be called guests). I am neither crew nor passenger, for the lecturer inhabits a strange but very pleasant 'Never Never Land', or should I say 'Never Sea'. The sea – there is nothing else like it on earth. It covers more than two thirds of our world, which should surely be more accurately named 'Planet Ocean'. It is a vast mirror held up to our personalities. The ocean has the power to return us to ourselves.

The lecturer's 'Never Sea' intensifies that experience. We spend many hours mingling with the guests, and in a typical voyage it is possible to become well-acquainted with as many as 100 souls. After the first lecture they all know the lecturer's name. It's quite a challenge for the lecturer to remember every one of theirs. Daily, over lunch and dinner, a lecturer faces the most earnest questions. There is no escape. The guest's experiences and stories enrich our own, and if lucky, the soul of the seascape can be captured like the green flash at sunset – but know your subject or you're soon found out! ●

Noble Caledonia takes travellers to spectacular destinations in the far flung corners of the world

"Seductive city of the north"

The cultural capital of Russia, St Petersburg, is often called the more poetical name of Palmyra

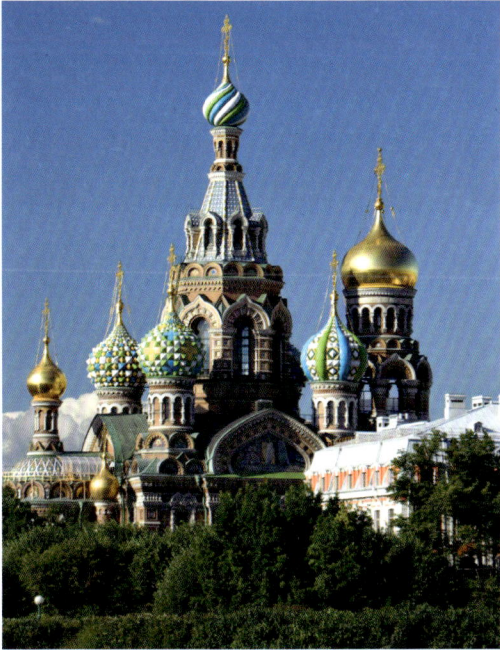

Our ship was sailing to Northern Palmyra – this beautiful, brooding city of the north. Once a great capital, it was founded to face the sea and the west. Arriving by water was the ideal way to realise its character. Military by history and military by tradition, it had in World War II suffered one of the most horrific events in world history; a perverted punishment for being the cradle of an ideology that 'shook the world'. Yet, as our ship eased its way along the river flowing through its centre, the early morning sun was celebrating its cultural and artistic essence. Always a city to evoke superlatives, it now swayed this beholder with its poetic interplay of water and stone, the majesty of its palaces, boulevards, grandiose squares, open spaces, slender bridges and lowering skies. Given its historical tragedy one grasps why some see it as oppressive and tragic, but to me on that glorious morning she emerged ethereal, magical, and miraculous. This seductive city has had many names during her 300-year history: St Petersburg, Petrograd, Leningrad. Nevertheless, its denominative, Palmyra, is the one that captures the mystery of its unique promise. ●

Acknowledgements

Thank you to all who took the time to dredge their memories for those brilliant, unforgettable moments when water – be it river, ocean or just the sight of it from dry land – made the world feel special, perhaps even magical:

Dame Margaret Anstee, Dame Joan Bakewell, Johnny Ball,
Jeremy Black MBE, Dr Alan Borg CBE, Peter Bowles, Rosie Boycott,
Hilary Bradt MBE, Sir Ranulph Fiennes, Anna Ford,
Frederick Forsyth CBE, Maggi Hambling CBE, Philip Hook,
Rachel Johnson, Quentin Letts, Jeremy Lewis, Maureen Lipman CBE,
Candida Lycett Green, Andrew Marr, Michael Palin CBE, Matthew Parris,
Tony Soper, Stephen Taylor, Colin Thubron CBE,
Admiral Lord Alan West, Sara Wheeler, June Whitfield CBE,
Ann Widdecombe, John Julius Norwich,
and HRH Prince Michael of Kent GCVO.

Thanks also to everyone at Noble Caledonia, James Pembroke Publishing and Just a Drop.

This book is dedicated to anyone who ever looked at the water and dreamed...